To

Bette, Brad, Brent, Chad, Craig and Pam
whose loving existence contributed to the
knowledge and experience represented by
this book

How To
Save Money
On Just About
Everything

By

William Roberts

Strebor Publications
Division of American Consumer Group Inc.
Laguna Beach, California

Published by Strebor Publications, Division of American Consumer Group Inc., P. O. Box 475, Laguna Beach, CA 92652

First Printing September 1991

Cover design by Linda Pinson

Library of Congress Catalog Number: 91-90901

Roberts, William.

How to save money on just about everything

ISBN 0-9629498-0-9

TABLE OF CONTENTS

TABLE OF CONTENTS

INTRODUCTION

"Certainly there are lots of things in life that
money won't buy, but it's very funny -
Have you ever tried to buy them without money?"
Ogden Nash

We all recognize the need to spend our money wisely. No one likes to pay more for an item than necessary. For some of us, it's a matter of saving for a special vacation, a long-cherished purchase, or a college education for our children. For others— especially those on a low or fixed income—it is more a matter of survival.

Whatever the reason, optimum management of his or her financial resources improves anyone's standard of living. Money saved on A and B leaves more to spend on C and maybe even allows the purchase of D as well.

Because of rapid changes taking place in consumer marketing, it is now possible for more people to save more money on more goods and services than ever before. And, thanks in part to the advent of the "information age," the average consumer is rapidly becoming more sophisticated in his shopping habits. Even so, there are still areas of savings available which many people don't know about.

In a letter to Lord Chesterfield, Samuel Johnson is quoted as having said "Knowledge is of two kinds. We know a subject ourselves, or we know where we can find information upon it." The purpose of this book is to not only add to the knowledge you already have, but to an even greater extent assist you in knowing where to turn for additional information.

A revolution in retail marketing has been taking place in the United States during the past few years, and is continuing. The major thrust of this revolution has been a growing shift away from the old distribution chain of manufacturer-distributor-wholesaler-retailer to systems that reduce the cost of getting the goods to the customer, and passing some of those savings on to him.

This upheaval in the marketing process has seen the creation and/or growth of such alternative sales channels as direct mail marketing, discount chains, clubs and warehouse stores, electronic marketing, and others. The number of organizations which sell to consumers at less than "list" price is growing rapidly.

To take advantage of the savings available from these retailers, you must know who they are and where to locate them. It is not possible, of course, to list all of them in a book this size. What this report does do is to list several of the major sources and give directions on how to locate many others. In addition, it contains pointers on how to achieve savings on items and services other than those normally purchased at retail shops.

Having the information in this volume at hand is not enough, in itself, to make your efforts at saving a success. To achieve this goal, you must become a practitioner of the "value-minded" approach to shopping. You do this by first training yourself to analyze *every* intended purchase. Do you have enough information about the product or service to make an intelligent decision? Have you decided that this is the model, type, size, etc. that you want or need? Would a different brand, or a model with fewer features, serve as well? How many vendors have you checked for price comparisons? Are there other sources which might be less expensive?

The second order of business, if you are to become a really savvy buyer, is to "know the market", that is, to be aware of what is available where and at what prices. Several chapters in this report will assist you in developing this capability.

Third, remember that the first price quoted is not necessarily the final price, and that more items are subject to negotiation than most people realize. You shouldn't haggle with the druggist over the price of a tube of toothpaste, or the green grocer over five pounds of potatoes (there are other ways to save on these), but there are numerous products and services which *are* susceptible to bargaining. Chapter 24 will help you improve your ability in this area.

Finally, you must consistently and conscientiously apply the information and pointers in this book to every buying situation. If you do this, you will soon find yourself mentally shifting into the mind-set of a savvy and competent purchasing agent on every transaction. You will also find yourself saving more money than you would have thought possible, and enjoying it! Consistent use of the data and suggestions contained in the following pages will enable you to fill your material needs with a significant savings in cost. The information is here—its up to you to make the most of it.

Chapter 1

HOME BUYING AND MORTGAGES

A home is the most expensive purchase most families will ever make. Consequently, it offers the buyer potentially the greatest savings he could ever achieve, especially when mortgage interest costs are taken into account. All costs in connection with buying a home should be carefully investigated and appropriate steps taken to keep them to a minimum. Ways in which this can be done are covered in this chapter.

There are three cost areas to watch in buying a home: the price of the dwelling itself; the closing costs (sometimes called settlement costs); and the cost ("points" and interest rate) of the mortgage. Each of these is addressed below.

TO BUY OR NOT TO BUY

Deciding whether it makes sense to buy your own home, determining whether you can afford to do so, and figuring out how much you should pay for it are all important questions which must be answered. The answers to these questions will vary from one individual or family to another, depending on financial and other considerations.

Mortgage companies and other institutions have established rule-of-thumb guidelines to use in estimating the ability of would-be buyers to meet house payments. The U. S. Department of Housing and Urban Development (HUD) gives these two: (1) The price of the home generally should not exceed two times your annual family income, and (2) A homeowner usually should not pay more than thirty-eight percent (38%) of income after Federal tax for monthly housing expense (payment on the mortgage loan plus average cost of heat, utilities, repair and maintenance. Local property tax should be included in these costs, although HUD doesn't mention it).

Of course, the would-be buyer must have the necessary cash to cover the down payment on the home plus all closing (settlement) costs, including "points" charged by the mortgage lender and possible pro-rated property taxes.

BUYING A HOME

After you have investigated all the angles, including shopping for available mortgage financing, and after calm and deliberate consideration have decided to pursue the purchase of a house, condo, apartment or town house, you should consider engaging a real estate broker to assist you.   A good broker can save you time by showing you only those properties that meet your specifications.   Brokers are also usually knowledgeable about schools, shopping centers, churches, and other items of interest in each neighborhood.

In selecting a broker, you should interview several until you find one that you have confidence in and feel comfortable dealing with.   Unless the property you end up buying is listed with this particular broker, the sales commission (which will be paid by the seller, not by you) will be split between your broker and the listing broker.

Caution: Bear in mind that even though you have engaged him to assist you, the buyer, your broker is going to be influenced to some extent by his own desire to make a sale and earn a commission, and by the interests of the seller.   From a legal standpoint, he is actually representing the seller (who is paying the commission) even though you asked him to work for you. In other words, its up to you to look after your own interests without placing too much reliance on the broker.

Inspect The Property: After your broker has shown you several properties and you have found one or more that suits you, you are ready to make the next move.   You should inspect each property carefully, from the street to the backyard, from the basement to the roof, and all places in between.   Look for any obvious defects such as inadequate insulation, wet floors, rotting wood, loose tiles, leaking toilet bases, loose caulking, broken windows, water spots on ceilings, etc. Ask about the ages of all appliances that will remain with the house, and any problems with them.

Make a list of all defects or problems encountered. This will come in handy if and when you begin negotiations. If you see anything that causes you to feel that a more thorough investigation by an expert is warranted, by all means have it done. It could keep you from buying BIG problems, or give you cause to make a bid considerably below the asking price. You can locate home inspectors by looking under Home Inspectors or Building & Home Inspection Services in the yellow pages of your telephone directory, or by contacting the American Society of Home Inspectors (ASHI), 3299 K Street N.W., Washington, DC 20007, telephone (202) 842-3096.

Making An Offer: Before you make an offer, your broker should be able to provide you with a computer printout showing all the homes in that area which are now on the market as well as those which have been sold over the past several months. This list will include full descriptions, asking price, and actual sales price (if sold). This latter information will give you a good indication of the actual market values in the neighborhood, which will assist you in determining how much your *initial* offer should be.

In starting your negotiations, don't let *anyone*—not the seller and not even your own broker—know that you or your spouse "really want" or "must have" that particular house. To do so will weaken your bargaining power beyond redemption. Many people make the mistake of asking the broker how much they should offer. This is a mistake—remember the points made earlier about the broker's relationship with the seller and his own desire to make a sale.

Look at the listing of recent sales in the area and note the average difference between asking and selling prices. If this difference has been running 5%, don't hesitate to offer 10% below the listed price. If your offer is not accepted and you are willing to go higher, you can always make a second—or third—offer. If the inspection report shows that more than a minimum amount of work would need to be done to put the house in good condition, deduct this amount from the figure you arrived at after taking off the 10%. After all, the owner of the house should have had this done before putting it on the market.

Before making your first offer, know the maximum amount you are willing to pay. Don't get caught up in a bidding war, or seduced into thinking that you must have this particular house at any price, or frightened that you won't ever be able to find another that you like as well. Any of these can turn what ought to be a calm and deliberate business decision into an emotional experience in which reason flies out the window—and with it any chance for price savings.

Additional Information: For more detailed information on home buying, write to the **Superintendent of Documents,** U. S. Government Printing Office, Washington, DC 20402 and ask for a copy of the U.-S. Department of Housing and Urban Development booklet *Wise Home Buying* (pub. HUD-267-H). The cost is $1.00 each.

A much more extensive treatise, which also covers things such as mortgages, home insurance, home improvements, taxes, and second homes is Consumer Reports Books' *How to Buy A House, Condo, Or Co-Op.* Check with your local library, or order a copy from Consumer Reports Books, 51 East 42 Street, New York, NY 10017 (price $14.95 plus $3.00 s&h).

CLOSING COSTS

Closing costs, called Settlement Costs in some states, are the costs which the seller and buyer respectively must pay at the time the sale/purchase "closes," or is finalized. These costs include several things, such as broker's commission, loan fees, insurance, taxes, title charges, title insurance, closing fee, lawyer's fees, recording charge, inspections, etc. etc.

As stated earlier, these costs are almost always higher than the buyer anticipated so it pays to obtain a reliable estimate of such costs in advance.

Earlier, we pointed out that one of the first things you should do after you decide to buy a home is to shop for mortgage financing. When you file your application for a loan, the lender is required by federal law to provide you with a Good Faith Estimate of the costs of settlement, and to give you a copy the booklet *Settlement Costs,* **a HUD Guide,** which explains in detail what the buyer may expect in the way of closing costs.

The HUD booklet mentioned above spells out your rights as a buyer under The Real Estate Settlement Procedures Act of 1974 (RESPA), and also contains much other information of interest to the potential home buyer. Rather than wait until you apply for a mortgage loan to get this booklet, we recommend that you order a copy from the **Superintendent of Documents,** U. S. Government Printing Office, Washington, DC 20402 (cost $1.50). The information in it will be useful in shopping for home buying services such as brokers, lawyers, and settlement services.

MORTGAGES

For the home buyer who finances his purchase, there is one cost even higher than the cost of the dwelling itself—his mortgage. For example, the interest costs on a 30-year $100,000 mortgage loan at a 10% interest rate is over $215,000, or more than twice the amount of the mortgage! Interest costs on the same loan at 11% interest over 30 years would be approximately $243,000—almost 2-1/2 times more.

These illustrations make it obvious how important it is to shop for the best mortgage terms when buying a dwelling. In the above example, a buyer who can negotiate a rate of 10% instead of a 11% would save $28,000 over the life of the loan! In addition, his monthly payments for principal and interest would be about $75.00 less, which might mean the difference between an affordable house and one that is not.

We will first consider the subject of mortgages in connection with acquiring a new home. Following that, we will show homeowners who presently have a mortgage and don't plan to move to a new home how they could effect substantial savings on interest costs.

Types of Mortgages: Escalating home prices and sky-high interest rates over the past several years have made buying a home in America, once considered an almost automatic God-given right, an increasingly difficult proposition. In response to this, there has been a bewildering increase in the types of financing plans available to the would-be home buyer.

Instead of just the common 20 or 30-year fixed-rate mortgage familiar during the first three quarters of this century, there are now Adjustable Rate Mortgages (ARMs), Rollover Mortgages, Balloon Mortgages, Graduated Payment Mortgages, and so on. The variations on these are almost endless.

It is not the purpose of this report to tell you, the reader, what type of mortgage you should have. Instead, we will show you where and how to get the information to make this decision yourself, and to point out the importance of fully understanding all the terms, conditions and implications of any financing plan being considered in order to save money on financing costs.

It is important that the person considering financing the purchase of a home be aware of the types of financing available, and understand the salient features of each plan. To this end, he should write to the **Federal Trade Commission,** Washington, DC 20580, and request a copy of *The Mortgage Money Guide*. There is no charge for this useful publication.

The foregoing publication includes not only descriptions of various types of financing, but points out the pitfalls to watch out for in each. In addition, payment tables showing the monthly payment amounts (principal and interest) for fixed-rate mortgages in various amounts over periods of 5 to 30 years are included.

These tables makes it very easy to compare the total cost of, say, a 9% versus a 10% $100,000 loan over 30 years, pointing out the extreme importance of shopping for and negotiating the best interest rate you can get.

One other point just as important to the borrower as the total financing costs is *understanding all the terms and conditions of the loan.* That means reading and comprehending the fine print. This is especially true of so-called "creative" financing, that is, anything other than the old-fashioned fixed-rate mortgage. Otherwise, the loan agreement may contain clauses that more than negate any savings the borrower thought he had obtained through shrewd negotiating. This point is so important that you should have a lawyer or a trusted banker friend review any loan document that you don't completely and thoroughly understand.

SAVING ON YOUR PRESENT MORTGAGE

Perhaps you already own your home which you financed under either a fixed-rate or ARM when mortgage rates were higher than they are now, and you are interested in (1) reducing your interest costs, (2) reducing your monthly payments, (3) increasing your equity, or (3) all of the above.

Refinancing Your Mortgage: One way in which this can be approached is to refinance your present mortgage. What this means, really, is to replace your existing mortgage with a new one carrying more favorable terms than the old one. This requires shopping and negotiating from the ground up, just as if you didn't have a mortgage. Because refinancing means incurring the same costs you ran into in taking out the original mortgage (application fee, appraisal fee, survey, mortgage insurance, attorney's fees, title search fees, inspection fees, loan origination fees, points, etc.), it is generally considered worthwhile to undertake this approach only if current interest rates are at least two percentage points lower than your present rate. Even then, it is considered to be worthwhile only if you plan to stay in your present home for another three years or longer. Otherwise you won't recoup the added costs of refinancing.

A Better Way: Even if you elect not to refinance your present mortgage, it is possible to save a considerable amount of money on interest costs while at the same time increasing your equity and reducing the term of your loan. This can be done entirely within your control without renegotiating your present loan, creating additional paper-work, or paying any fees or commissions!

These worthwhile goals can be accomplished by using an almost painless method known as pre-payment. For example, if you have a $100,000 mortgage carrying a 10% interest rate, by adding as little as $31.13 per month to your current mortgage payment, you could save up to $43,000 in interest charges over the life of the loan and reduce the loan term by five years! Up the pre-payment to $87.45 per month, and you could save up to $84,000 and cut the time by 10 years!

Note that these additional payments are not *costing* you anything. They represent money you would have to pay in any event, but by paying them early you reap the benefits of reduced interest costs faster equity buildup, and shorter loan life.

(**Note:** Some mortgages have a clause restricting early payment—check with your lender if you are not sure about yours.)

More information on this subject can be found in a book entitled *A Banker's Secret*, by Marc Eisenson. Every present or potential mortgage holder should borrow a copy of this book from his local library. If your library doesn't have a copy, the book is available from Good Advice Press, Box 78, Elizaville, NY 12523. Credit card buyers may call (914) 758-1400. Price of the book is $9.95 (plus $2.50 s&h).

In addition to explaining in fully understandable terms the concepts and results involved in pre-paying loans, it answers many questions about the subject and includes a glossary of mortgage terms, pre-payment tables, debt reduction tables, mortgage factor tables, interest calculation formulae, and other useful information.

Chapter 2

FOOD AND HOUSEHOLD SUPPLIES

An American household of four people spends an estimated $5000 to $10000 per year on groceries and miscellaneous household supplies. The actual amount for each family varies, depending on factors such as income, tastes, food habits, and locality. Whatever the amount, it is possible with some planning and a bit of effort to cut these expenditures by 10% to 15% or more. This is equivalent to getting a salary increase (after taxes) of $500 to $1500 per year—many, many times the cost of this report!

It is not our intent to tell you what to eat—everyone has their own preferences on that—so you will not find any menus here. We will, however, show you how to save money on your grocery bill and still eat as well or better than you now do.

Money savings on food purchases are accomplished by paying attention to four basic areas: planning, shopping, preparation, and avoiding waste.

OVERALL PLANNING

The first step in planning is to make a chart which you might call a "Preference Guide." This is simply a list, broken down into breakfast, lunch, dinner, and snack columns, in which you list those things which members of your family like. It will cover foods from your family's usual eating patterns, but should also include other items which are overlooked because of habit, or because you just don't think of them while shopping. This is not a shopping list, but is to be referred to as a reminder when preparing your shopping lists.

Menu Planning: With this list in hand you are now ready to start meal planning by making a menu for each meal of the day. It is recommended that this be done for one week at a time, unless you have already determined that a different time frame is better for you.

Meal costs depend, among other things, on the types of food included in the menu. Chicken, for example, costs less than a beef roast. You can (and should) make this type of comparison for many food items as you go along, but let us first develop a cost savings plan which will apply to whatever type food you buy.

As you make your menus for the first week's meals, look at those items which you can make in quantities large enough for another meal or two to be served later that week or frozen and served at another time. Beef roasts and ham served for dinner, for example, make excellent sandwiches for lunch the next day or two. Pasta left over from a main course one day can become a salad for a later meal. And most foods can easily be frozen for later use—either after they are cooked, or prepared for cooking then divided, with a portion going into the freezer before cooking.

Seasonal supply and availability should be taken into account for fruits and vegetables when planning your menu. Prices are lowest when supply is greatest, which means at the height of the growing season or at harvest.

Planning Your Shopping: After you have planned your menus for the week, you are ready to make a shopping list. When the list is completed, check it against the contents of your pantry, fridge and freezer. Cross off any items which you already have on hand.

The quantity to be purchased for each item on your list should be determined by (1) the amount needed for the planned meals, (2) any planned excess amount for later meals, (3) the unit size or sizes available, (4) its perishability, and (5) quantity price breaks. Buying a large quantity might be cheaper than buying a small one, but if some of the excess ends up in the garbage disposal due to spoilage it may actually be more costly.

SHOPPING

Where you choose to shop can have a major impact on food costs. You should select one or two conveniently located supermarkets for groceries and, if there is one in your area, one warehouse store for other household supplies such as cleansers, paper products, and similar items.

Individual item prices can vary as much as 20% or more from one store to another. However, running from store to store to buy advertised "specials" can actually cost you money (and time) unless the stores are near each other. It is better to find out which market in your area is the consistent "low price leader" and do the bulk of your shopping there.

There is a simple way to determine whether a store consistently offers lower prices *for the items you buy* than others. Some newspapers carry price comparisons of local markets based on a hypothetical bag of groceries. This may or may not be applicable to you and your purchases. It is better to do your own price comparisons, because the things you normally buy probably won't match the newspaper's shopping list.

At the end of this section is an example of a chart used to compare prices between supermarkets. You can use this to make up one of your own. The first column lists items which you normally purchase on a regular basis, the second column provides space for brand name or other identification, and column three is for the unit in which the item normally comes, such as gallon, pound, dozen, etc. The columns following are for prices at each of the stores you check. You should cover at least three supermarkets or other stores, if there are that many convenient to you. It is suggested that you do the price comparison exercise once a month for two or three months. Chances are you will find that one particular store consistently has a lower overall total price column for the items you buy. If so, this is the one you should stick with. Do an up-date of the price comparison chart thereafter every six months just to see if any major change has taken place.

In making price comparisons, don't overlook store brands, generic foods, or bulk items. Many people are so conditioned by advertising that they automatically buy well-known brand names when other choices at much lower prices would be acceptable. If you fall into this category, try one or more of the other selections to see whether it is acceptable. The price difference is often substantial.

We have just recommended against running around town to take advantage of advertised specials. However, specials at the store or stores where you plan to shop anyway can be an important source of price savings and should be taken into account in planning (or modifying) your menus. When it is possible to do so, using manufacturer's coupons to purchase store specials will result in larger savings -- and greater yet if you catch a special on which "double" coupons apply.

COUPONS

Coupons are discount certificates issued by many manufacturers to induce consumers to buy a particular product. According to Carolina Manufacturer's Service, Inc., more than 270 *billion* coupons with a redemption value of $135 billion were issued in the USA during 1989. This amounted to approximately $1500 per household. Average face value of the coupons issued was 49.7 cents. Products covered included a myriad of canned, frozen and packaged foods, plus dozens of other household needs such as cleaning supplies, paper products, batteries, cosmetics, medicines, and others.

There are probably very few people who don't know what manufacturer's coupons are and who don't receive a supply at least once weekly via their mailbox or in supplements to their Sunday newspaper. However, surprisingly few people take full advantage of the savings which they afford. Only about $3.5 billion in coupons, less than 3% of those issued, are redeemed each year, according to CMS.

It is obvious from the low redemption rate that a great many people are unaware of the significant savings possible with coupons, or else they feel culling, clipping and using them is too much trouble. Even a savings of 10%—and more is possible—is worth a little bother. For example, a random sampling by the author using 18 coupons on the day this was written resulted in price savings of 4% to 51%, with the average being 12%. A 12% savings on annual expenditures of $5000 would net $600 which could be used to buy other things—or put into a savings account.

Establish A System: To take advantage of coupon savings, it is necessary to establish a system and stick to it. Below are some guidelines used by savvy coupon shoppers.

* **Review your coupon supply sources—newspaper supplements, magazines, direct mailings by distributors, door-to-door handouts, or whatever—to determine that you have a good and steady supply. If not, increase it by taking one or more Sunday newspapers (just a couple of coupons will reimburse you the cost of this).**

* **Set aside thirty minutes or so at a specified time each week for clipping and organizing. Enlist other family members to help you, especially children. Cut out only those coupons which you can use for the items you plan to buy to meet your household shopping list, or which you can trade to others. Don't get trapped into impulse buying just because you can get a discount. This could wipe out any savings you make on your normal list. If you have friends who collect coupons for items different than what you purchase, work out a swapping arrangement with them.**

* **Organize your coupons according to your own system: by food type, alphabetically, by grocery store section -- whatever you find works best for you. Put them in a folder or envelope near wherever you make out your shopping list. Use them together with the "preference list" mentioned previously in working up your grocery list, then take them with you to the market and use them. After a short while it will become an automatic habit and the savings will flow naturally.**

* **Make price comparisons between brands and between sizes. Unless you have a strong brand preference for an item, choose the**

one that has the lowest net price *with or without* a coupon. Sometimes the brand which has the coupon is so costly that it is still higher than an acceptable competitive brand even with the discount. Also, be alert to *unit* price—that is, price per ounce, gram, or whatever—instead of just the price per box or jar. Unit prices are shown on the shelf by most supermarkets. Surprisingly, the "giant economy size" often costs more per unit than the smaller sizes. Since coupons specify "cents off" rather than a per-centage, savings are usually greater on the smallest size you are allowed to buy.

For a more thorough explanation of the advantages of "coupon savvy"—and how to go about obtaining and using it—order one (or both) of the following booklets:

The New Coupon & Refund Encyclopedia, by Jan Leasure. Send a check or money order in the amount of $3.50 (includes postage) to Jan Leasure Books, P. O. Box 639, Libertyville, IL 60048.

Coupon and Refund Guide, by June Lee Scott. Price $4.00 including postage. Order from Tell View Corporation, 640 North Greece Road, Suite, 268, North Greece, NY 14515.

REDUCE WASTE

Spoiled foods and leftover scraps put down the garbage disposal represent a major area of potential savings. Almost everyone could reduce food purchases from one to three percent or more by reducing wastage. Following the few simple rules below will help you do this automatically.

* **When shopping for perishable foods, buy only amounts that can be used while they are still good. Buying in larger quantities just because you get a low price is no bargain if you end up throwing part of it away.**

* **In buying meat, bear in mind that an expensive lean cut may be more economical than one which requires you to throw away excessive bone, gristle or fat.**

* Unless you purposefully plan to freeze or refrigerate the surplus, prepare only enough food for a given mean. Cool and then refrigerate or freeze any surplus immediately after the meal. Use refrigerated foods as soon as possible, preferably within two or three days. Clean out your refrigerator weekly to make sure you are not accumulating food that has spoiled, and to make room for new leftovers.

* When shopping, check the "sell-by," "use by," and "best-if-used by" dates shown on many items. Choose the one that shows the latest date. Don't buy anything that has an expiration date sooner than you expect to use it.

HOUSEHOLD SUPPLIES

Non-food household supplies such as cleansers, detergents, furniture polish, floor wax, paper and plastic products, mops, brooms, etc. may be less expensive at warehouse stores or discount chains than at local supermarkets. As pointed out elsewhere, you may have to buy in larger quantities than normal to get this price break. Because packages or lot sizes may be larger, in order to make price comparisons it will be necessary that you calculate the unit price (i.e., price per ounce, quart, piece, or whatever). Larger quantities will mean more money tied up in inventory, but fewer trips to the store will be required in the future.

INFORMATION SOURCES

If you need help in menu planning, or if you would just like to have ready access to many types of recipes without spending a fortune on cookbooks or magazines, go to your local library. It will have dozens of books featuring recipes from many cultures, as well as some of the popular food magazines.

You can copy those recipes which you try and like, and if you wish you can keep a constantly revolving supply of cook books on hand. And, don't forget the food section of your local newspapers. In addition to recipes, tips and advertised specials, these are a source of discount coupons. For a detailed guide

on obtaining the best in food values, you may order a booklet
entitled *Your Money's Worth In Foods* (Home and Garden
Bulletin Number 183) from the Superintendent of Documents, U.
S. Government Printing Office, Washington, DC 20402.
Enclose a check or money order for $2.35 with your order.

For two-person households, the same source will send you the
booklet *Thrifty Meals for Two: Making Food Dollars Count*
(Home and Garden Bulletin Number 244). The price for this
publication is $2.50.

PRICE COMPARISONS: FOOD & HOUSEHOLD SUPPLIES

ITEM	DESCRIPTION	UNIT	STR #1	STR #2	STR #3
Milk	_____	____	_____	_____	_____
Eggs	_____	____	_____	_____	_____
Butter	_____	____	_____	_____	_____
Rice	_____	____	_____	_____	_____
Beans	_____	____	_____	_____	_____
Spaghetti	_____	____	_____	_____	_____
Bacon	_____	____	_____	_____	_____
Sausage	_____	____	_____	_____	_____
Hamburger	_____	____	_____	_____	_____
Cheese	_____	____	_____	_____	_____
Tuna	_____	____	_____	_____	_____
Flour	_____	____	_____	_____	_____
Sugar	_____	____	_____	_____	_____
Coffee	_____	____	_____	_____	_____
Lettuce	_____	____	_____	_____	_____
Celery	_____	____	_____	_____	_____
Onions	_____	____	_____	_____	_____
Potatoes	_____	____	_____	_____	_____
Oranges	_____	____	_____	_____	_____
Detergent	_____	____	_____	_____	_____
DW Soap	_____	____	_____	_____	_____
Paper towels	_____	____	_____	_____	_____
Plastic bags	_____	____	_____	_____	_____
TOTAL:			_____	_____	_____

[Note: Example only. Your list should reflect the items you buy.]

Figure 1

Chapter 3

HOUSEHOLD UTILITIES

At monthly bill paying time its not unusual for the family member charged with this chore to make some comment about the size of the telephone bill, or grumble about the high cost of electricity, gas or water. If it is implied that some other family member is responsible for this state of affairs, a heated discussion often follows these remarks.

In the interest of family harmony—as well as family economics—this chapter lists practical steps which anyone can take to reduce the cost of telephone service and other household utilities.

SAVING ON TELEPHONE CALLS

If you have noticed (and how could you avoid doing so) ads in the printed media, over TV and via direct mail by the major long distance telephone carriers, you may have gained the impression that the amount of your telephone bill is determined primarily by which long distance company you use.

The LD business is fiercely competitive, with discount programs and rates changing fairly rapidly. The company that is lower in price today may not be tomorrow. While there may be some price difference between LD carriers, the total amount of your bill can probably be reduced more by following the pointers in this chapter than by changing phone companies.

LD carriers have discount programs for inter-state (and in some cases intra-state) toll calls. If you make an hour or more of long distance calls per month on average, and don't subscribe to the plan offered by your present carrier, it will probably be worth your while to check out their discount plan.

Comparing Rates: It is fairly easy to compare rates. Take one of your typical monthly bills. The places you called will be listed, along with the date, time of day, minutes spent on each call, and the charge for the call. Copy this information on to a sheet of paper, leaving space to note the day of the week beside each date, and columns for cost-per-minute for your phone company and any others you plan to compare.

Calculate the cost per minute of each call on your bill. Then call the other long distance carrier or carriers. Obtain their basic monthly rate and information on any special charges or discounts. Now ask what their charge per minute would be for each of the cities on your list *for the day of the week and time of day* indicated. If you subscribe to a discount plan from your present carrier, use comparable information from the other carriers you compare.

Add up the columns and compare the totals. Unless the numbers are significantly different, choose the company with which you feel most comfortable. Plan to achieve your telephone savings with the tips given below.

Incidentally, your experience in collecting the above information may have helped you decide which company you would rather use—or, more likely—which company or companies you prefer *not* to use. Whether the line was always busy when you tried to call, the attitude of the people you talked to, and the degree of difficulty in obtaining the information you wanted are pretty good indicators of the type of service you could expect from that company if you ever had problems or a complaint.

Use 800 Numbers: The number of businesses which have 800 toll-free numbers is growing by leaps and bounds. The reason is simple -- they have learned that it helps business. Most of these organizations—especially those dealing in direct mail or featuring products on TV—advertise their 800 numbers. What most consumers don't realize is that there are many others, including companies that don't market directly to consumers, that have toll free numbers.

Before calling *any* business long distance, you should check and see if they have an 800 number. You can contact the 800 directory assistance operator by dialing 1-800-555-1212. For frequent users of long distance, AT&T publishes two directories of 800 numbers, one called the Consumer Edition ($9.95) and the other the Business Edition ($14.95). These may be ordered by calling 1-800-426-8686.

800 Numbers for Travelers: Scott American Corporation, Box 88, West Redding, CT 06896 publishes an eight-page pocket-size brochure called *The Phone Booklet* which contains toll free numbers of interest to travelers. These include car rental agencies; hotels, motels and resorts; hotels/casinos; buses and airport limousines; charge cards; auto clubs; trains; airlines; vacation rentals; cruise lines; tour operators; and tourist information offices. The brochure is free, but there is a shipping and handing fee of $2.00 for single copies, or $3.00 for up to 10 copies. Larger quantities are available, but larger S&H fees apply.

Don't Use Personal 800 Numbers: Some telephone companies are now advertising residential 800 numbers for people who have a child away at school, a relative living away, or who travel a lot and would like to call home frequently without the hassle of using a credit card. At the time this report went to press, the cost of the cheapest such service was $5.00 per month and twenty-five cents per minute for each call. This is not cheap. You would probably be better off to keep on using your LD calling card number—and letting your relatives use it, also, if you are so inclined.

Don't use 900 Numbers: One of the biggest sucker games going at present, in the view of this author, is the 900 number scheme in which telephone callers have to pay a fee per minute *in addition to the telephone company charge*. Charges run from one dollar to $50 per *minute*. Callers are spending $1 *billion* dollars per year on these calls. Conversations with sensual-sounding females, dubious credit card pitches, talking to psychics, listening to—or giving your own—"romantic confessions," questionable "sweepstakes" award notifications and similar gimmicks are being pitched at TV audiences on a daily basis.

Some of the truly crooked rackets using this system have it rigged so callers are put on hold (or have to listen to extended sales pitches) for long periods of time while the minute meter clicks merrily along. Others charge for a minimum number of minutes regardless of the duration of the call.

If you get the urge to call a 900 number, think twice. In all probability, practically any reputable company you want to do business with has an 800 toll-free number. Even if it doesn't, why should you pay for more than just a normal telephone call to do business with them?

On the Road: When traveling, don't charge intra-state calls to your hotel room. Unlike inter-state calls, hotels and motels can stick hefty surcharges on in-state calls. If you are traveling in a foreign country, be even more careful. Hotels in many foreign countries are notorious for their "service" charges for long distance calls. Go to the local postoffice or other public phone booth to place your overseas calls—or make arrangements in advance for the other party to call you.

Miscellaneous Phone Tips: Following are a few more pointers to help you reduce your phone bill bulge.

  * One way to lower your telephone bill is to use the phone less. When practical, write instead of calling.

  * Long distance carriers charge less during specified hours at night, and also on weekends and holidays, than during normal business hours, so try to make LD calls during these periods. Check with your carrier to find out the times and days which apply in your case.

  * Before making a toll call, get organized before picking up the telephone. List the points to be covered in your conversation on a piece of paper, then go through the list in a business-like manner when you get your party.

* If you call a place of business and the party you want to speak to is not available, leave your name and number and ask that he or she call you back. After all, you paid for one call to reach them. Why should you pay for another?

* Use your telephone directories whenever possible rather than calling information. Directory assistance calls add up.

SAVING ON ENERGY USE

Following is list of pointers on ways to save on energy costs in the home. This can be used as a check-list. Go over it and check off those things which you are *not* doing now. These are the areas in which you can save money. Savings can be significant. Don't be surprised to find that with a little effort and changing of habits you can achieve savings from 10% to 20% or more.

Heating Pointers: Almost half of household energy costs go for heating and cooling, so this is the area of largest potential savings. Here are ways to utilize that potential in your heating bill:

* **Keep out air leaks. Caulk and weatherstrip windows and doors if necessary. This and the following pointer apply to cooling as well as heating.**

* **Have your insulation checked by an expert. Add more if necessary.**

* **Keeping heating equipment well maintained. Have furnaces serviced at least once each year.**

* **Install a clock-operated thermostat and set it to automatically lower the temperature at night.**

* **Insulate accessible heating ducts.**

* Lower your thermostat to about 65 degrees during the day and 60 (or below) at night. If necessary, wear a sweater or light jacket to keep warm.

* Keep windows and doors near thermostat closed. Cool air in this area will make your heater work overtime.

* Check duct work for air leaks. Seal leaking joints with duct tape.

* Clean or replace filters every month heating system is in use.

* Make sure attic access door is tightly closed.

* If you have radiator heating, clean surfaces frequently.

* Keep draperies, blinds and shades open on the sunny side of the house. Close them at night.

* When using your fireplace: lower thermostat setting to 55 degrees, close all doors and warm air ducts leading to the room with the fireplace, and crack open a window about one inch in the fireplace room to provide air supply.

Cooling Pointers: In areas where air conditioners are used several months of the year, electricity charges for cooling are often higher than heating in the winter time. The following pointers will help reduce those charges.

* Keep cooling equipment well maintained.

* Consider installing a house ventilating fan for use when the outside temperature is cool.

* Set your thermostat as high as comfortably possible. 78 degrees is recommended for acceptable comfort and energy savings.

* Clean or replace filters at least monthly.

* With window air conditioners, use an electric fan to spread the air further.

* Turn off window air conditioners when you leave the room for long periods of time.

* Keep all sources of heat away from the thermostat.

* Keep out daytime sun with awnings, drapes or blinds.

* Use lights as little as possible. They generate heat.

* Cook in early morning or late evening to keep from heating up the house.

* Open windows instead of using the air conditioner on cooler days.

Kitchen Energy Savers: Your kitchen is a big energy-use area. If you're not already doing so, practice the points below.

* Use a cover when boiling water. It will heat up much faster.

* Turn off electric stove burners several minutes before specified cooking time. The retained heat will keep on cooking.

* When using the oven, cook several dishes at the same time. Use a timer. Don't open over door frequently.

* Use small electric pans or ovens for small meals.

* Use pressure cookers or microwave ovens. They use less energy.

* Cook on top of the stove instead of in the oven when possible. Top burners use less energy than ovens.

* Use dishwasher only when full. You will wash fewer loads this way. It takes as much energy to wash a small load as a large one.

* Let dishes air dry. Washer heating elements gobble up energy.

* Keep refrigerator compartment set at 38 to 40 degrees and freezer compartment at 5 degrees. A separate freezer unit should be set at 0 degrees.

* Make sure refrigerator door are tight. Replace seal if necessary.

* Don't open refrigerator or freezer door more than is necessary.

* Defrost manually-controlled refrigerators regularly.

Laundry Pointers: These simple steps can save physical as well as electric energy.

* Wash only full loads, or adjust water level for smaller loads (if washer equipped with variable level controls).

* Wash clothes in warm or cold water and rinse in cold.

* Don't use more detergent than necessary.

* Presoak badly soiled garments.

* Fill clothes dryer (but don't overload). Overloaded machines don't dry efficiently.

* Keep dryer lint screen and external exhaust clean. Again, this is a matter of drying efficiency.

* Dry clothes in consecutive loads at one time rather than waiting until later for additional loads. This makes use of heat retained in the dryer.

* Use automatic dry cycle if your dryer has one.

* Dry light and heavy garments in separate loads.

* In good weather, use an outside clothesline. You'll not only save energy, you'll like the way your clothes smell.

* Remove clothes that will be ironed from the dryer while still damp.

Lighting Pointers: To lighten your energy bill make it a point to:

* Turn off lights in rooms not being used.

* Install solid state dimmers or high-low switches.

* Use fluorescent lights where possible.

* Keep 3-way bulbs on lowest setting when not needed for reading.

* Use outdoor lights only when they are needed. Use a photo-electric cell, sensing device or a timer for outside night lights.

* Convert outside decorative gas lights to electric.

EQUIPMENT AND APPLIANCE POINTERS

Shop more carefully when buying home devices, and use the following pointers to help select energy-efficient equipment.

* When buying any home appliance or other energy-using equipment, compare energy ratings and buy the most efficient.

* Compare operating costs. Under federal law, manufacturers are required to put labels showing estimated operating costs on the following items: furnaces, water heaters, refrigerators and freezers, air conditioners, heat pumps, clothes washers, and dishwashers.

* If you plan to use electric heating, consider a heat pump instead of an electric furnace.

WHEN BUILDING OR REMODELING

By following these steps when you are building or remodelling, you will save a lot of money down the road.

* **Insulate walls and ceiling as recommended for your area (consult building products companies or your local utility company for the proper "R" factor).**

* **Insulate floors over crawl spaces, cold basements, and in rooms above garages.**

* **Install windows which can be opened.**

* **Use double-pane glass in windows and glass doors.**

SAVING ON WATER

Saving on water usage is not only wise from an economic view point, in sections of the country faced with severe drought conditions it is essential. The following pointers will help you achieve this end.

* **Deep soak your lawn when you water it, and water less often. Light watering evaporates and does little good.**

* **Water lawn and plants only when needed. Don't leave sprinklers on automatic during cool or rainy periods.**

* **Water in early morning to reduce evaporation and prevent fungus growth. Just before sunrise is the best time.**

* **Don't water your patio, the street, or gutters. Adjust sprinklers to spray water where needed. Don't water when its windy.**

* **Set lawn mower blades one notch higher than usual to reduce evaporation in lawn.**

* Use mulch around trees and shrubs to cut down on evaporation.

* Check all pipes, hoses and faucets for leaks. Replace washers or make repairs where needed.

* Use a bucket of soapy water to wash car. Use hose only for rinsing.

* Don't let children play with hose or sprinklers.

* When landscaping, plant drought-resistant plants and trees.

* Cover swimming pool when not being used to reduce evaporation.

* Clean driveway and sidewalk with a broom instead of washing them down.

* Check toilets for leaks. Put a few drops of food coloring in the tank. If the coloring appears in the toilet bowl (without being flushed), you have a leak that needs repairing.

* Don't run water while shaving or brushing your teeth. Use a little warm water in bottom of basin for shaving.

* Use a water-saving shower head and take shorter showers.

* When showering, wet yourself down then turn off the water while you are soaping. Turn water back on for rinsing off.

* When bathing in the tub, take a shallow-water bath. Half a tub instead of a full one reduces water usage by 50%. It also takes less water than a normal shower.

* While waiting for hot water to arrive at any location, catch the cold water in a bucket and save it for cooking or watering plants.

* Put a plastic bottle filled with sand or gravel in your toilet tanks. Keep these objects away from tank operating components.

This will reduce the amount of water used each time the toilet is flushed.

* Don't use the toilet as a waste disposal mechanism for cigarette butts or other debris. Every flush means up to seven gallons of water goes needlessly down the drain.

* Use your dishwasher and clothes washer only for full loads. This saves energy as well as water.

* When washing dishes by hand, don't leave water running when you rinse. Instead, use a container of clean water.

* Wash vegetables in a pan of clean water instead of letting the faucet run.

* Keep a bottle of drinking water in the refrigerator. You will then have cold water to drink without having to let the faucet run until the water comes out cold.

* Defrost frozen food by taking it out of the freezer and letting it set out (or use your microwave). Don't run hot water to defrost.

OTHER SOURCES

More information on this subject can be obtained by calling the customer service department or customer information desk of your local utility company. Almost all utility companies have helpful printed literature which they will send free of charge. Many of them will also do an "energy audit" of your home and provide you with specific recommendations free of charge.

You can obtain the booklet *Tips for Energy Savers* at no charge by writing to the Technical Information Center, U. S. Department of Energy, Box 62, Oak Ridge, TN 37831.

A detailed publication on how to make energy-saving home improvements, *In The Bank...or Up The Chimney*, is available from the Superintendent of Documents, U. S. Government Printing Office, Washington, DC 20402.

Chapter 4

BANKS AND BANKING

Almost anyone who deals with a bank—which is just about everyone—overpays banks several thousands of dollars during his or her lifetime. This happens because many people hold banks in a sort of awe, as if they were special institutions endowed with some mystical power, and because a great many people have the mistaken impression that bank fees, policies, and procedures are not only fixed but are standard throughout the banking world.

SHOPPING FOR A BANK

A bank is a business. It is in the business of selling a product (loans), and providing services in the form of storing and transferring money via savings and checking accounts. As with any other business, banks have competitors. And, like other businesses, they have a price list (interest rates, fees, etc.). To carry the analogy further, a bank's prices may be subject to negotiation, just as in other businesses. Even in cases where prices are not negotiable, they are certainly open to *comparison.*

Shopping for a bank, whether to open a checking or savings account or to apply for a loan, should be approached in the same way as shopping for anything else. Determine what it is you are shopping for, then make up a list of the features to be priced and compared.

Many banks offer a variety of accounts to fit individual needs. One type may be free of service charges but not pay interest, another may pay interest but require a minimum balance, yet another may charge for each check drawn on the account, or limit the number of free checks.

To attract clients, many banks offer ancillary services to regular customers at no charge or at reduced prices. These may include safe deposit box rentals, notary service, free traveler's checks, a membership in a discount buying club, etc. Others may offer a free gift of some sort for opening an account. In comparing banks for the purpose of opening an account, emphasis should be placed on recurring items such as interest credits or payments, service charges, etc. rather than on one shot gifts. This is where your money will be spent (or saved) in the years to come.

CHECKING ACCOUNTS

In shopping for a checking account, you should obtain information on types offered by at least three banks. This will permit you to make direct cost comparisons between the banks. A suggested form for collecting this data from each bank is included at the end of this chapter.

Your selection should be based on your own banking activity, that is, the average number of deposits made and checks written each month, the amount of money you anticipate keeping in the account (high, low and average), and other features such as automated teller service, free traveler's checks, free notary service, etc.

Checks: Most banks charge their customers for checks for use with their checking accounts. Some of them provide a limited quantity of checks free to new customers as an inducement for opening the account, with subsequent checks provided at an established price. While it is news to many people, a depositor *is not required* to buy or use checks offered by his bank. There are commercial check printing companies that sell printed checks, guaranteed to be accepted by the customer's bank, at prices which are usually considerably lower than the bank charges.

Two of these check printers are listed below. Both offer checks in many designs. Prices quoted are for normal single checks and were current at time of writing, but you should verify before ordering.

Checks In The Mail, 5314 North Irwindale Avenue, P. O. Box 7802, Irwindale, CA 91706, telephone (800) 733-4443. $4.95 for 200 checks.

Current, Inc., P. O. Box 19000, Colorado Springs, CO 80935-9000, telephone (800) 426-0822. $4.95 for 200 checks.

SAVINGS ACCOUNTS

As recommended for checking accounts, collect data on all savings accounts available (if more than one is offered) from at least three banks. Most banks have two or more types, one usually called a "regular savings account" and another a money market account named a "liquid CD" or something else to distinguish it from an ordinary savings account. The latter will probably pay a different rate of interest and have different rules for withdrawals, opening amount, minimum balance, and so forth.

The major points to be covered are (1) minimum opening balance (if any), (2) rate of interest the account will earn, (3) the effective annual yield, (4) minimum operating balance (if any), (5) whether there is a service charge if the account falls below a certain balance, and (6) whether there is a penalty (and its amount) for early withdrawal.

ACCOUNT INSURANCE

Whether for a checking account or savings account, make sure the bank you choose is insured by the FDIC or the FSLIC.

BANK LOANS

This relates to bank financing other than mortgages, which are covered in Chapter 1. When shopping for money, that is, looking for a loan to finance the purchase of a car, furniture, or other personal item, take the same approach you would in shopping for anything else. Shop around, collect the information needed to make a thorough comparison, then negotiate.

If you are a member of a credit union, you should start there on your loan shopping expedition. CU interest rates are almost always lower than a bank or Savings & Loan, and loan conditions are often less onerous as well.

If you don't belong to a credit union and already have an established relationship with a bank through existing accounts, by all means include that bank in your shopping list. But don't stop there. Go to at least two more banks and/or S&L's. At each of them, explain to the loan officer that you are shopping for a loan, and that you would like to receive a proposal from his bank.

The loan officer may ask you to fill out a loan application prior to discussing details. Whether or not you do this is up to you. It really isn't necessary until you decide at which bank you want to apply for the loan. You should, however, provide him with enough information to determine whether you would be apt to qualify if you did apply. This would be assurance to him that spending time to answer your questions would not be a waste.

Your Loan Shopping List: Take along a note pad with your questions already written down. These should include the following as a minimum:

[1] What interest rate would apply? Would collateral be required? How much? In what form?

[2] Is there a fee for processing the loan? Are there any other charges?

[3] Is there a grace period for late installment payments? If so, how long?

[4] Is there a late charge for payments not made on time? If so, how much?

[5] Would there be a penalty for early repayment of the loan? If so, how much?

When you have analyzed the information gathered from the banks, you are ready to approach the bank which appears to have the best deal. Remember, you are not a supplicant begging for a favor but a potential customer discussing a business arrangement which, if concluded, would be beneficial to both parties.

Negotiate: For consumer loans, bank interest rates will be comparable but not necessarily identical. Even if the bank with which you have chosen to negotiate has quoted a rate below that of other banks, try to obtain a further cut of 1/2 or 1/4 point. Certainly do this if their quoted rate is the same as the other banks.

If your credit rating is good, you may well get the reduction. This is especially true if you have (or are willing to open) other accounts at the bank. The loan officer will know by now that you have talked to his competitors, and he will want to keep you as a customer (if you are one), or get you to "move over" if you're not. If you have a certificate of deposit or other funds on deposit at the bank which you plan to leave intact during the life of the loan, determine whether the bank will lower their loan rate if you use those funds as collateral. Many of them will.

In today's climate, banks are looking for good solid loan prospects after having gotten badly burned in recent years by poor ones. If you don't succeed in obtaining a lower rate, try for a change in one or more of the other conditions mentioned above.

SENIOR CITIZENS

If you are in the Senior Citizen group (this ranges anywhere from age 50 or 55 and up, depending on the institution), there are some special deals to be had at banks and S&L's. See Chapter 25 *Special Deals for Senior Citizens* for more information.

CHECKING ACCOUNT DATA SHEET

Name of Bank_____

Contact_____

Location_____

Phone_____

Account name_____ Is it interest bearing?_____

Is there a service charge? (Y) (N). If yes, how much_____

Are balances required? (Y) (N). If so, complete the following

        Opening $_____

        Minimum   _____

        Average   _____

Is there a limit on transactions? How many per month?_____

Amount charged per additional transaction_____

Does the account provide overdraft protection? (Y) (N). If so,
how much is the fee for this?_____.

Which ATM networks do you belong to?_____

Is there a charge for using your ATM? (Y)(N). Amount_____

Note any other charges or limits in connection with this type of
account_____

List any other services offered free of charge to holders of this type of
account:_____

_____

Are you a member of: FDIC [ ] FSLIC [ ]

Note: Complete one of these data sheets for <u>each</u> type of account at
<u>each</u> bank (survey at least three banks).

Figure 2

Chapter 5

CREDIT CARDS

Credit cards may be a bane or a blessing, a nuisance or a convenience, a disaster or a pleasure, depending on how they are used. Regardless of what else they may be, they *are* a way of life in the United States of America so it behooves the cardholder to know as much as possible about this modern tool of consumption financing.

As mentioned in the banking section of this report, during his lifetime the typical American consumer spends literally thousands of dollars which could be saved on bank fees and interest charges. This includes the use of credit cards. It does not include millions of dollars ripped off each year by con artists working various credit card-related scams.

The information in this chapter will help you select the credit card or cards which best fit your needs at the lowest cost to you. Implementation of the suggestions in this chapter alone could save you many times the cost of this book every year from now on!

OBJECTIVE

Too many people have wallets bulging with plastic. A large number of credit cards represents greater exposure to loss or theft, more bills to be paid, extra book-keeping, and potential confusion. It also often indicates that the cardholder has not read the fine print and thoroughly analyzed the terms and rates for each of the cards, so he could be paying a king's ransom in fees and interest charges without even being aware of it.

As we shall see, each type of card has its own features, good and bad. There are further advantages and disadvantages for individual cards within each category, related primarily to fees, interest charges and benefits offered.

You should adopt as your objective a plan to retain the convenience of credit cards, reduce exposure to loss or theft, AND save hundreds of dollars on fees and interest charges. A reduction in wallet thickness and pocket bulge will likely be welcome by-products.

How Many Cards? To reach this objective, your strategy should be to have the fewest number of cards to serve the greatest number of needs at the lowest possible cost. Because everyone has different needs, or at least different views on those needs, the exact number of cards held by individuals may vary.

TYPES OF CARDS

Let us take a look at the differences between the major types of cards. This should make choosing our bare-bones inventory of cards fairly simple.

There are three basic types of credit cards in predominant use: (1) company credit cards issued by individual firms such as oil companies, major department stores and other retailers which may be used only at the stores of the issuing firm; (2) so-called travel and entertainment ("T&E") cards such as American Express, Diners Club and Carte Blanche; and (3) financial institution-related cards, often referred to as bank cards. VISA and MasterCard are the major cards in this field .

The Discover card of Sears Roebuck is a sort of hybrid between (1) and (3). At the time of this writing, Sears has announced plans to issue a new no-fee Visa card. Sears is already the largest single issuer of consumer credit cards, according to the Nilson Report of Santa Monica, California, with 38 million Discover Cards and 70 million Sears charge cards.

If Sears goes ahead with its no-fee Visa, it will no doubt have a major impact on financial institutions which charge an annual fee. These banks are already feeling the effects of the AT&T "Universal" MasterCard (800-662-7759), another no-fee entry.

J. C. Penney has entered the fray with its JCPenney National

Bank Preferred Visa Gold and Gold MasterCards (800-622-5789).

Company Credit Cards: These cards are normally valid only for use at one of the stores, gas stations, or other outlet of the issuing company. Most of them allow a grace period of 20 to 30 days for payment of the total amount charged before assessing an interest charge (sometimes referred to as a late-payment charge, finance charge, or other name). No matter what it's called, it is usually a hefty annual percentage applied to the unpaid balance.

It is not unusual for the APR (annual percentage rate) charged on these cards to run 18% to 22% or even higher. If you are the sort who regularly pays these types of charges within the grace period, you are avoiding the high interest charges. However, you still may have the problems of bulging wallet, extra bill paying, and additional bookkeeping.

If, on the other hand, you don't pay the full balance monthly and use these as a type of revolving credit, you are in all likelihood paying more in interest charges than you need to. Most retailers (including oil companies) which issue their own credit cards will accept other major credit cards. Inasmuch as you can obtain a bank credit card which charges lower interest than the typical department store or oil company, you might be better off destroying the company card and obtaining a lower-interest bank card.

Travel and Entertainment Cards: T&E cards such as American Express and Diners Club might be considered convenience cards rather than credit cards because they require the full balance due to be paid within 30 days of statement date. They do not charge interest during this 30 day period but may suspend the account if payment is not received on time. If payment is not received within 60 days of statement date, they charge a penalty which may be a minimum charge of $10 to $15 or 2-1/2% of the balance due, depending on the amount of the balance.

T&E cards offer additional features in the way of product warranties, rental car insurance, travel insurance, etc. These cards might be suitable for many consumers who use cards for convenience only. However, they charge an annual fee. If you pay your monthly charges in full you could save the cost of the annual fee by obtaining a "no fee" bank card. The only good reason to use a T&E card would be if it offers benefits of importance to the user not available under one of the other cards.

Bank Cards: The major bank credit cards, Visa and MasterCard, are so called because until fairly recently they were issued only through or by banks and other financial institutions. Although other organizations are now promoting them, the overwhelming majority are still issued by banks (AT&T's recent Universal Card entry may change this) and—like other bank services—have a wide range of fees, interest rates and conditions, depending on the issuing institution.

WHICH CARD TO USE?

In order to keep credit card expense at a minimum, selecting which issuer to use will depend on whether you intend to pay off the balance in full each month or whether you expect to use the card as a means of financing monthly installment payments. If you plan to pay in full every month, you should select an issuing company that has no annual fee. If you plan to carry a credit balance, your first priority would be for a card that has the lowest interest rate, with the annual fee being a secondary consideration.

Credit Card Information Sources: There are cards available to meet both cases, and there are services which make it easy to locate and compare information on hundreds of issuers. Some of these services are:

Bankcard Holders of America, 560 Herndon Parkway, Suite 120 Herndon, VA 22070. Telephone (800) 638-6407. BHA publishes a *No Annual Fee List* (cost $1.50) consisting of banks across the country that offer credit cards with no annual fee. It also publishes *BHA's "Fair Deal" Banks*, banks across the nation with interest rates of 16.2% and below ($1.50); *Report on Gold Cards* ($5.00); and *Report on Secured Cards* ($3.00). These reports may be purchased by the public for the prices indicated, or may be obtained at no charge by BHA members. The annual membership fee is $18.00 and includes a newsletter and other reports and services not listed here.

Consumer Credit Card Rating Service, P. O. Box 5219 (Ocean Park Station), Santa Monica, CA 90405. Telephone (213) 392-7720. This organization sells its *Credit Card Locater Kit* for $17.00. This lists over 1300 Visa and MasterCard rates by institutions in all 50 states. Interest rates, annual fees, and grace periods are shown. It also provides information on American Express, Diners Club, Carte Blanche, Discover, JCP and Air Travel Card. Included in the kit is a credit card cost "Calculator;" a "Comparer" which looks at cost factors other than interest rates; and, the "Informer" which has information on various credit card benefits.

Ram Research/Publishing Co., Box 1700 (College Estates) Frederick, MD 21701. Telephone (301) 695-4660. For $5.00, Ram Research will send you its *Consumer Packet* which includes its *National Survey* listing of banks and savings institutions which offer lower interest rates on bank credit cards nationally, and its *Low Rate Survey*. The national survey also lists no annual fee issuers, low interest rate premium or gold cards, secured cards, and other cards. The low rate survey list contains 400 to 500 institutions, ranked from the lowest interest rate to the highest. Annual fees, grace periods and telephone numbers of listed institutions are shown.

ALL THAT GLITTERS

During the past several years issuers of credit cards have increased their annual take considerably by appealing to the vanity of their customers. By exploiting snob appeal, they have raked in billions of dollars peddling cards designated as "Premium," "Gold," or "Platinum" at annual fees of $35.00 to $300.00. This is reportedly the fastest growing segment of the market, which says a great deal about the gullibility of the American consumer. This fast growth rate, however, may be its own undoing. The implied status bestowed by a gilded card starts to fade when waiters and gas station attendants see them by the dozen every day.

Other than the perception of status, the sales pitches for these cards revolve around (1) high credit limits, and (2) additional service features. Neither of these is a very solid reason when compared to other cards available. Most consumers have no problem in spending as much money as they can afford on an ordinary non-premium card. If the credit limit is not high enough, most credit card issuers will gladly increase the users credit line to an amount consistent with his ability to pay. And anything beyond this is financially unhealthy, anyway.

As for additional benefits, you should first determine which (if any) of these are really of value to you. Chances are you won't use most of these so-called enhancements, and those that are important are probably available with other cards.

AVOID CREDIT CARD SCAMS

The fringes of the credit card market is populated with dubious characters who fleece the unwary of millions of dollars each year. The basic operating mode of these operators is to promise (or imply) that they will help obtain a major credit card for people with poor credit or no established credit. They advertise in newspapers, use direct mail, or leave brochures at the counters of retail establishments. Some have begun advertising on TV, urging suckers to call in using a 900 number which the applicant pays for by the minute!

These operations have two things in common. They ask for money up front to process an application, and they all offer "guaranteed credit," regardless of your income level or credit history. Avoid these pitches. If you want a credit card and need to establish, or re-establish, your credit you can do so by contacting one or more of the issuers of "Secured" credit cards whose names you can obtain from one of the credit card listing services mentioned earlier. You will still be required to place a deposit with the institution, but you *won't* have to pay an application processing fee! And you won't get ripped off.

SUMMARY

If you are not already doing so, you can save considerable money in the use of credit cards by following the few simple rules below:

* Use a maximum of two bank cards, one "no annual fee" card for those charges you intend to pay in full each month, and one "low interest rate" card for bills you want to pay in installments.

* Choose cards which have a grace period (the period of time before interest charges start accruing) of *at least* 24 days.

* If you do a lot of traveling or have unusually large business expenses, *one* only T&E card might be a good investment for you, even though it carries an annual fee, but check it out. It might not be necessary after all.

* Forget the so-called premium cards. You will have no trouble spending all the money you want with a plain old charge card. If you do, have your credit limit increased.

* Read all the fine print in any credit card agreement. Ask questions if you don't understand all the clauses. Some hefty penalty charges can be buried here.

* Avoid con artists. Deal only with recognized institutions. Don't pay any money up front to anyone for the privilege of filing a credit application. *Don't* call a 900 number to apply for a credit card.

Chapter 6

INSURANCE

The American consumer is faced with the perplexing problem of needing (or, in some cases, being required to have) more and more insurance as rates for many types of coverage sky-rocket. Ambulance-chasing lawyers, award-happy juries, and inadequate legal safeguards have made ever higher liability coverage a necessity while at the same time forcing premium rates higher and higher.

Financial responsibility laws in some states now require all motorists to carry a minimum of automobile liability coverage, regardless of premium rates. Ever-spiraling medical and hospital costs have forced insurance companies to jack up health insurance premiums. Laws and mores which allow an individual to be less and less responsible for his own actions—regardless of how stupid or careless they may be, but blame (and sue) someone else—have lead to the well-earned description of this generation as the "litigious society." The effect on liability insurance premiums has been horrendous.

Total insurance premiums for an American family will typically run between $2000 and $5000 per year, with costs tending to be higher in metropolitan areas and states with high populations. A savings of just 5% to 10% in overall premium costs is a worthwhile goal. The following comments and suggestions should help you accomplish this.

First, a few comments which apply to all forms of insurance.

HOW MUCH INSURANCE?

How much insurance to carry in each category should be based on the amount necessary to protect your assets and life style, taking into account that by accepting the highest deductibles you can absorb without too much difficulty results in lower premium costs.

WHICH INSURANCE COMPANY?

Regardless of the type of insurance, it is safer to buy a policy from a company rated A or better (A+ is the highest) by the **A. M. Best Co.** insurance rating service (Ambest Road, Oldwick, NJ 08858), or a comparable rating from one of the other recognized rating organizations. A rating by Best can be obtained by calling (900) 420-0400, but it is cheaper to write. Calls cost $2.50 per minute. Callers must have the insurance company's identification number. If you don't have this ID number, it can be obtained by calling another Best office at (908) 439-2200.

Other rating services are provided by **Duff & Phelps Inc.**, 55 East Monroe St., Chicago, IL 60603; **Moody's Investors Service**, 99 Church St., New York, NY 10007; **Standard & Poor's Corp.**, 25 Broadway, New York, NY 10004; and **Weiss Research**, 2200 Florida Mango Rd., West Palm Beach, FL. 33409.

THINGS TO AVOID

You should avoid buying individual policies with narrow coverage such as mortgage loan insurance, flight insurance, single disease coverage; policies pitched on TV by celebrities or ex-celebrities; and auto rental insurance *if you are properly covered under your own auto policy.* One possible exception to this general rule is broad based accident insurance (AD&D).

Rather than a bunch of policies carrying very limited coverage, you will save money by purchasing broad-based coverage under comprehensive policies. Your health insurance should cover *all* diseases; your disability coverage should be sufficient to replace your regular income; life insurance should be adequate to pay off your bills without buying separate credit insurance; and your auto insurance should cover you when driving *any* vehicle, including rental cars.

The fixed-payment policies flogged on TV by present or former movie or TV personalities are usually inadequate and cost much more per $1000 of coverage than mainline insurers. Your premium money could better be spent on a plan from one of the higher-rated companies.

SHOP AND COMPARE

We repeat again: Before making any major purchase, and this certainly includes insurance, shop around. Make a list of the specific coverage wanted and request quotations from three or more sources. Make sure the companies quoted are in one of the top-rated groups. Then compare each feature, benefit, and cost. Don't let the agent or company include "extras" at an additional cost that you don't want or need.

ACCIDENTAL DEATH & DISMEMBERMENT INSURANCE

This type of policy limits coverage to loss of life or limb as a result of certain specified accidents. The range of accidents and scope of coverage varies greatly from one company to another, so shopping and comparing is important. If your employer offers this coverage in it's group insurance package, the rates will probably be far lower than you could obtain on your own. Although AD&D insurance is limited in coverage, it can be a useful part of your insurance portfolio—especially if you can't afford as much life insurance as you would like and want to partially supplement it—as premium rates are much lower than life term or straight life insurance.

AUTOMOBILE INSURANCE

Auto policies normally include coverage for personal liability, collision and comprehensive, uninsured (and underinsured) motorists, and medical payments. Other coverage is available from some companies as options. These include towing expense, loss of use (rental car reimbursement), and personal injury protection, among others.

Liability coverage is the most important part of your auto policy. The amount of coverage should be large enough to protect you against financial hardship—or even disaster—in the event of a lawsuit. Fortunately, fairly large incremental increases in the amount of coverage do not increase premium costs in the same proportion. Liability coverage of 50/100/25 ($50,000 per person/$100,000 per accident/$25,000 property damage) could probably be increased to 100/300/50 for about a 25% increase in premium.

Minimizing Premium Costs: One way to keep auto insurance costs as low as possible is to carry the highest deductible you can on the collision and comprehensive portions of the policy. These are the parts of the policy that cover replacement or repair costs to your own vehicle resulting from collision or events such as fire, theft, vandalism, and storm. When obtaining quotations, ask that deductibles of $300, $500 and $1000 be quoted. Note the difference in premiums then decide which you would feel more comfortable with.

Another way to save is to purchase a car which has a low loss rate for repair costs and theft. These carry lower premium costs. A list showing standings in this area is available free of charge from any **Allstate Insurance Company** office.

Many insurance companies grant discounts for such things as cars equipped with air bags or automatic front-seat belts, cars equipped with anti-theft devices, more than one car insured by the same owner, people with good driving records (no accidents or traffic tickets within a given period of time), drivers participating in car pools, drivers who have completed a defensive-driving or high school driver training course, senior citizens, farmers, and good students. When obtaining quotations, request a list of the things for which each of the companies will allow a discount and see how many you qualify for.

Check The Coverage: When comparing quotations, determine whether the policies cover your liability when driving a rented vehicle. The one you purchase should have this coverage. If not, you can still beat the high cost of CDW (collision damage waiver) charged by auto rental companies by charging the rental on one of the credit cards which provide this coverage free of charge. As of this writing, this includes American Express, MasterCard Gold, and Visa Gold. Check with the issuer of whichever card you have to make sure this is still valid before relying on it to cover you.

Choosing An Insurer: If you don't know where to start in selecting the companies to compare, you might commence by referring to the October 1988 issue of *Consumer Reports* which you should find at your local library. It carries information on a number of companies. The premium costs listed will now be out of date, but you can still use them as a guide to selecting the companies you want to contact.

HOMEOWNERS AND RENTERS INSURANCE

These plans cover losses of or to your home and/or personal effects from a variety of things, ranging from fire and storm to vandalism and other causes. Like automobile insurance, they may also contain liability coverage. Renters (tenants) policies usually cover only personal effects as tenants do not own the property in which they live.

If you are a homeowner, you should by all means include enough liability coverage to protect your assets, even if this means buying additional coverage under an "umbrella policy." You should also opt for a feature called "guaranteed replacement cost" which means the insurance company will pay the full cost of repairing or replacing the property in event of loss. Otherwise, you may end up getting far less than this if you have a claim and are deemed to be underinsured.

As with auto insurance, the higher the deductible you are willing to accept, the lower the premium cost. Premium cost may also be reduced if you buy coverage from the same company carrying your auto insurance. Most policies have low limits of coverage on jewelry, currency, art objects, etc. Obtaining adequate coverage may require that you "schedule" these items individually and pay an additional premium. In shopping for homeowners (or renters) insurance, be sure to read the fine print and note the exceptions.

When comparing policies, **note the limits of coverage and the exceptions on other items as well.** Basic coverage varies widely from one provider to another. Coverage not included can often be added for a small additional cost.

HEALTH INSURANCE

Often referred to as Hospitalization & Medical Insurance, health insurance is one of the most important and increasingly costly forms of insurance coverage. By far the best way to save money on health insurance is to belong to a group plan offered by an employer or other organization to which you belong. Plans offered by employers (and other qualified groups) provide more coverage at less cost than individuals can purchase on their own.

Don't Overlook Disability Coverage: If at all possible, include Disability Insurance in any health policy bought. This is just as important as life insurance for those who depend on their monthly income to live (and this includes most of us). A disability plan should provide coverage to replace about 60% to 75% of the insured's monthly salary, as disability benefit payments are not subject to U. S. income tax (unless Congress changes the law subsequent to this writing), *provided the premiums are paid by the insured and not by the employer or other group organization!*

The Disability Insurance policy should cover the insured *until such time as he has recovered sufficiently to return to his former occupation.* Some plans provide coverage only until the disabled party is recovered sufficiently to do *any type of work.*

Disabled people who qualify may also obtain Social Security disability benefits, which helps make up the difference between insurance benefits and their former salary.

Health Coverage Alternative: If you are not eligible for any type of group coverage, health insurance will be very costly to obtain. All you can do is shop and compare cost and coverage. You should also obtain quotations from Health Maintenance

Organizations (HMO's) in your area. These are groups that provide specified medical services to their members at a fixed yearly cost.

Medicare Information: People with Medicare who have questions about their coverage under this program, or who would like information on possible supplemental insurance, may request the free booklet *Guide To Health Insurance for People with Medicare* from the U. S. Department of Health and Human Services, Health Care Financing Administration, Baltimore, MD 21207.

LIFE INSURANCE

There are two basic types of life insurance, term and whole life. Term insurance policies are issued for a certain amount of coverage over a specified period of time. At the end of that time, they expire and coverage ends. Whole life policies (sometimes called straight life or permanent life) remain in force for the insured's life time, subject to the conditions in the policy. There are many other life insurance policy names employed in the insurance industry, but they are all a form of either term or whole life.

Because the basic form of term insurance is simply insurance and nothing else, and because it does not offer features such as cash value build-up, dividends, etc., it is the lowest priced life coverage available. Many insurance advisors recommend this type policy for people who simply want insurance protection, and who look to other avenues for their investments and/or savings.

How Much and Which Type?: The amount and type of insurance a person should buy are personal decisions dictated by his or her own circumstances, plans and preferences. For help in making these decisions, we suggest you obtain a copy of *A Consumer's Guide to Life Insurance*, published by **American Council of Life Insurance**, Community and Consumer Relations, 1001 Pennsylvania Ave., NW, Washington, DC

20004-2599 (tel. 800-423-8000). There is no charge for this booklet, which was published by the Council in cooperation with the Extension Service of the U. S. Department of Agriculture.

Comparing Policies and Prices: When you have decided on the type and amount of insurance wanted, it is time to shop and compare. Considering that there are almost 2000 life insurance companies in the U.S., this could be a daunting undertaking. Fortunately, in the field of life insurance, there are folks who will gather the necessary information for you.

These are quotation services who will send to you *at no charge* complete price information from a range of companies on the plan of your choice. Their only requirement, which is a fair one considering the service rendered, is that you buy whichever policy you select through the company which provided the quotations to you.

Following are the names and addresses of four of these quotation firms:

InsuranceQuote, 3200 N. Dobson Road, Bldg C, Chandler, AZ 85224 (telephone 800-972-1104);

LifeQuote of America, Inc., 25 S.E. 2nd Avenue, Suite 1100, Miami, FL 33131 (telephone 800-776-7873);

SelectQuote Insurance Services, 140 Second Street, San Francisco, CA 94105 (telephone 800-343-1985);

TermQuote Services, Inc., 3445 S. Dixie Drive, Suite 130, Dayton, OH 45439-2303 (telephone 800-444-8376).

For More Information: For a more detailed discussion on Life Insurance, you may refer to *Life Insurance: How To Buy The Right Policy From The Right Company At The Right Price*, by The Editors of Consumer Reports Books with Trudy Lieberman. Check your local public library, or order from Consumer Reports Books, 51 East 42 Street, New York, NY 10017.

Chapter 7

TAXES

It is not the intent of the author nor the purpose of this report to undertake the role of tax advisor. Tax questions should be referred to a qualified tax advisor or tax attorney. However, since this is a book about how to save money, and since approximately forty percent of our collective annual income goes to pay taxes in one form or another, it is appropriate that we point out areas of taxation which you should explore for possible savings.

There are some taxes about which nothing can be done except pay them. One example is Social Security taxes. If you are employed—whether by others or by yourself—and have an income, you have to pay the mandated social security tax.

There are other taxes which may be avoided, delayed or minimized. This chapter will briefly summarize some of these and tell you where to find additional information on the subject.

INCOME TAXES

Federal and state income taxes fall into the category of taxes which cannot be avoided, but which often can be reduced with proper planning. This subject is so immense that a dozen books the size of this one (even if we were tax experts, which we're not) would not adequately cover it.

For assistance in this area, we suggest that you refer to one of the current income tax publications. We stress "current" because the rules, regulations and interpretations in this field are in a constant state of change. If you have any questions or doubts on points covered in any of these publications, you should consult a qualified tax advisor.

See whether one of your local libraries—public, college or special—has one or more of the following available. If not, check out the inventory at a good bookstore.

Arthur Young Tax Guide, Peter W. Bernstein, editor. Published by Ballantine Books.

Consumer Reports Books Guide to Income Tax Preparation, published by Consumer Reports Books, a division of Consumer's Union.

H&R Block Income Tax Guide, published by Collier Books, MacMillan Publishing Company.

J. K. Lasser's Your Income Tax, prepared by the J. K. Lasser Institute, published by Prentice Hall Press.

Smart Money Moves for the 90's by the editors of *Money* magazine, compiled and edited by Junius Ellis. In addition to tax-saving strategies, this book covers several other areas of interest to consumers.

PROPERTY TAXES

Many people complain about the size of the tax bill on their home or other real estate which they own—especially when taxes are increased due to a reassessment program or for some other reason—but few realize that there may be something which they can do about it.

Analyze your property tax statement. Look at the assessed value of the property, the items specified in the bill (such as additional levies for improvement bonds, flood control bonds, school bonds, and so forth). Make sure all such additional items apply to the area in which you live. Government employees *can and do* make mistakes. If there is an item you're not sure about, call the tax collector's office and question it.

Check on the assessed valuation assigned to your property, especially if you don't feel it is correct or fair. Find out what valuations have been placed on similar properties in your neighborhood. You can do this by talking to owners of the properties, or by going to the courthouse and checking the records yourself.

If you determine that similar properties carry lower assessments, follow prescribed procedures for protesting your assessment. The tax collector or county court clerk can tell you how to go about this. Enough such protests are successful to make this worth investigating.

Some states have programs allowing for reduced taxes for veterans, the disabled, low income families, or for dwellings used as a principal residence (homestead). Inquire whether your state has such programs and determine whether you qualify for one or more of them.

If you are including payment of property taxes with your monthly mortgage payment (as many people do), check to make sure that you are not over-paying. Some lenders collect an excess monthly amount which they later "adjust" when establishing the following year's payment schedule. In the meantime, they have interest-free use of your money at your expense.

SALES TAXES

Sales taxes can usually be avoided by purchasing items out of state via mail order catalogs, electronic shopping, etc. (see Chapters 18 and 19). We say "usually," because this is not always the case. For example, if the vendor has a retail establishment located in your state, it may be required to charge the applicable sales tax for your state even though the merchandise was ordered and shipped from outside your state of residence.

Taxes on a vehicle purchased in one state and registered in another cannot be avoided. When the buyer goes to register it in his state of residence, applicable state taxes (sometimes called a "use" tax) will be slapped on at that time. In California, a monstrous smog tax will be added on as well—even if the vehicle was manufactured to meet the California vehicle smog requirements and is so certified! This bill obviously was passed to protect the state's automobile dealers rather than the environment.

ESTATE AND INHERITANCE TAXES

Probably the saddest taxes of all are the federal estate and state inheritance taxes which are assessed upon a person's property at the time of his or her death. We use the description "saddest" because these two taxes together can take away almost half of a person's estate. They often are not given any thought until there is a death in the family, but if proper planning had been undertaken while the deceased was alive, these taxes could have been significantly reduced or even avoided completely!

Not only can estate and inheritance taxes be avoided or reduced, the costly, frustrating, and time-consuming chore of probate can be eliminated completely or made of little significance. Lawyer's fees, which can be exorbitant even on the probate of modest estates, can be greatly reduced or eliminated.

The solution to the foregoing problems is a perfectly legal device known as **The Living Trust**. You may have seen newspaper advertisements for seminars on living trusts, or lawyer's ads for "consultations." We suggest strongly that you read a good publication on this subject before spending money on seminars or lawyers. By doing so, you will have learned the things you need to know in order to save time and money when you do take the necessary step of hiring a lawyer to draw up a Living Trust and complementary Will.

The clearest and most comprehensive book we have read on the subject of Living Trusts and related subjects is entitled *The Living Trust, The Fail-Proof Way to Pass Along Your Estate to Your Heirs Without Lawyers, Courts, or the Probate System,* by Henry W. Abts III (published by Contemporary Books). If your local library doesn't have this book (or one similar), or cannot get it for you, by all means buy one at a bookstore even if they have to order it in for you.

Proper estate planning can save literally hundreds or thousands of dollars, depending on the size of the estate; more importantly, it can save untold time and hardship for those who have to administer the estate.

Note: We consider the foregoing suggestions on trusts and wills to be among **the most important** made in this book! Not only can you make sure your that the bulk of your estate goes to your heirs instead of lawyers and tax collectors, you can save them untold days, weeks or months of frustration and wasted time.

Chapter 8

CAR BUYING AND LEASING

Other than a home, buying a car is probably the single most expensive purchase the average American family makes. And for most people it is repeated several times during his or her lifetime. Many people dread shopping for a car more than going to a dentist, and for good reason. In too many cases purchasing a motor vehicle can be a frustrating and bitter experience.

BUYER BEWARE

Automotive marketing has gained a reputation over the years—deservedly so, unfortunately—that would have caused almost any other business to clean up its act years ago.

False advertising, high pressure selling, "switch and bait" tactics, implied threats, price jacking, contract doctoring, manipulating interest rates, overcharging for service policies, slipping unwanted insurance coverage into the contract, outright lying, and sundry other shady or dishonest actions have been the order of the day in this business for too many decades.

Used car salesmen are perceived by many people as being more villainous than new car dealers, and although there probably are car dealers who do not engage in any of the shoddy practices described above, the would-be buyer has no way of knowing which are the good guys and which the bad until it is often too late. As emphasized throughout this report, the buyer's best protection is **knowledge**—and the courage to use it!

BUYING A NEW CAR

Before beginning your shopping expedition to dealers showrooms, decide which car model you want, and the options desired. You must have this information in order to find out what the dealer's approximate cost is, and therefore what price you can reasonably hope to negotiate. Make up a worksheet which shows the model of the car at the top and lists the desired options down the left hand side. Opposite each item (including the base car model), have space for two columns, one headed "Sticker Price," and another titled "Estimated Dealer Cost." As noted below, the dealer's cost probably will not be the same as "invoice price."

Sticker Price: The Sticker Price (sometimes called the Monroney Sticker) appears on a label affixed to a car window. This is required by federal law. It shows the base price, options installed by the manufacturer (with suggested resale prices), and manufacturer's freight charges. There is usually a supplemental sticker which shows the retail price of any options installed by the dealer, and an item called ADM (additional dealer markup) or ADP (additional dealer profit).   This information goes in Column One of your worksheet.

Invoice Price: This is the price billed to the dealer by the manufacturer *before any rebates, allowances, discounts or incentive awards*.   It is probably *not* the dealer's actual cost which is almost always lower than that shown on the invoice. The invoice price includes freight (sometimes called destination and delivery charges), so be alert to any attempt by a dealer to add this charge on again.   This price information is useful as a comparison against the estimated dealer's cost, which you can obtain from sources listed below.

Some dealers may be reluctant to show you their invoice, but if they have advertised to sell at "one hundred dollars above invoice," or something similar, they can't very well refuse your request to see it.   Or, if you have obtained dealer's costs (see below) and the salesmen challenges your figures, demand that he prove you wrong by showing you his invoice! If you are unable to see the invoice, you can still make a very close estimate of dealer's cost and this is the important figure from a negotiating standpoint.

Dealer's Cost: This is the net cost to the dealer after rebates, allowances, incentives and bonuses from the manufacturer. There are two types of sources for obtaining dealer cost information: publications which you can buy (or find in your local library), and computer printouts obtained from service organizations which provide such printouts to your specifications for a fee. The following publications include manufacturer's suggested retail prices *and* dealer's costs:

MARKET INFORMATION

A few years ago, getting adequate knowledge about car prices, advertising, and sales practices would not have been possible. In today's "information age," that is no longer true. Listed in this chapter are a number of sources for obtaining the price information you will need in negotiating the best possible deal.

Publications: The following list provides a wide selection in types of publications and price ranges.

Consumer Guide (Year) Cars (Signet Edition), Publications International, Ltd., 7373 N. Cicero Ave., Lincolnwood, IL 60646, Tel. (708) 676-3470. Price $8.95 (plus $1.50 p&h).

Dealers Costs for (Year), Dealers Costs Inc., P. O. Box 1312, Waco, TX 76703. Tel. (817) 757-2277 Price $13.00 (American Cars); $12.00 (foreign cars).

Edmund's New Car Prices, Edmund Publications Corp. West Hempstead, NY 11552, Tel. (516) 292-0044. Price $24.00 per year (3 American and 2 foreign issues).

Kelley Blue Book New Car Price Manual, P. O. Box 19691, Irvine, CA 92713, Tel. (714) 770-7704. Subscription $79.00 per year (6 issues).

Computer Printouts: There are a number of services which will provide a computer printout showing dealer's costs on specific car models, including costs on options specified by the customer, for a fee. Following is a partial listing:

AutoVantage, 3355 W. Alabama St., Houston, TX 77098-1718 Tel. (800) 999-4227. Limited number of printouts free to members annually, small charge for additional printouts. Membership fee $49.00/yr. Members receive other services & discounts, including a network of dealers which sell new cars to members at pre-arranged discounted prices; fleet pricing at participating Goodyear and Firestone service centers; 10% maintenance discounts at other participating dealers, and used car valuations. (trial memberships available).

Car/Puter, 1603 Bushwick Avenue, Brooklyn, NY 11207-9916 Tel. (800) 221-4001, Price $20.00 plus $2.00 p&h per report

Consumer Reports Auto Price Service, Box 8005, Novi, MI 48050, Tel. (313) 347-5810. Price for one car $11.00, two $20.00, three $27.00, each additional $7.

Your Own Computer Printout: If you have a personal computer, you might be interested in a software program called **"Cars"** published by Lifestyle Software, 63 Orange Street, St. Augustine, FL 32084 (tel. 800/289-1157 or 904/825-0220). This program not only gives the estimated dealer's cost on more than 650 auto models, but includes detailed specifications, features, and options for the various models. With Cars, you can specify any combination of features or options and the program will list all vehicles meeting these criteria.

The Cars software program sells for $39.95 and may be updated twice a year for an additional fee.

Prices By Telephone: Members of the American Automobile Association can use the AAA Auto Pricing Service to obtain information on either new or used car prices by telephone. The charge to members for this information is $9.95 for one vehicle, $17.95 for two, or $25.95 for three. Non-members can also use this service, but their costs are $2.00 more than it is for members. When calling AAA, have your Visa or MasterCard number ready. Telephone (800) 933-7700. This service is available in the lower 48 states only.

FINANCING AND TRADE-INS

In addition to price information on the car itself, the potential car buyer (new or used) should go shopping for financing *before* he goes car shopping, unless he intends to pay cash. If he has a car to trade in, he should determine it's market value in advance (see comments under **Buying A Used Car** (below).

GET WRITTEN BIDS

After you have shopped for financing and determined the value of your trade-in (refer to later sections in this chapter on these two subjects), you are ready to start your rounds of the dealers.

It is important to pin down the price of the vehicle *before* talking about financing, service contracts, or trade-ins. Tell the sales person you are going to get quotations from at least three dealers, and you want his best price in the form of a written bid. The bid must cover all accessories and any other applicable charges. The salesman will probably come up with several reasons why he can't give you a written bid, or will try to convince you that it is not in your interest for him to do so, or that his best "deal" is one you have to accept on the spot. All of which is nonsense.

If the sales person is reluctant to give a written bid or doesn't deal with you in a straight-forward business-like manner, tell him you are going to consider only those dealers who have submitted their offers in writing *and mean it!* If he is still reluctant to cooperate, walk out and don't come back. You are the potential buyer, so you have control of the situation. All you have to do is exercise it.

After prices for the car, accessories and related charges have been written down, you can ask that a service contract be added to the bid as a separate item if you want it. Bear in mind that service contract prices are often jacked up by the dealer, so be sure and compare these between dealers and with outside sources. Keep all the specifications on the bids for all dealers exactly the same so you will be able to make direct comparisons.

Don't let the salesman drag a trade-in allowance into the transaction at this point (see the discussion later in this chapter regarding trade-ins), and don't let him add *any* type of insurance to his bid. You're shopping for a car, not insurance. Buy your insurance from a broker or insurance company. (See Chapter 6 *Insurance*). This takes away one more gimmick the salesman can use to flim-flam you on the car price (not to mention on the insurance premium).

Negotiating the Deal: After you have obtained at least three bids, you are ready to select a dealer and begin negotiations. You may choose to go to the dealer with the lowest bid or, if the bids are close in price, may elect another dealer because of their service reputation, your own confidence factor, the way they treated you during your first visit, or whatever.

Upon returning to the dealer you have chosen, you should ask for the sales person who gave you the written bid. You should then make an offer below the bid price. The amount of the offer should be slightly above dealer's cost as shown by the information you have collected. From this point, you would proceed as in any negotiation, with discussion and offers back and forth. The maximum price you should be prepared to pay is the amount of the written bid you have already obtained. You should be able to better this in most cases, unless your choice is a popular car that is in short supply.

If the salesman says he has to "check with the boss," or someone else, tell him you are interested in talking only with someone authorized to make a deal and if the salesman can't do that, please get you someone who can. *Don't* get put in the position of being whiplashed between two or more people. Do your negotiating with one person only. If the dealer won't agree to this, or if he tries any other of the myriads of tricks auto salesmen have cultivated over the years, get up and walk out. If you make it quite clear that you won't put up with any nonsense, this probably won't occur, but if it does go to the next dealer on your list and start again.

AUTOMOBILE LEASING

Generally speaking, it is almost always more expensive to lease than to buy. However, if you are interested in exploring the possibility of leasing a car, we suggest you obtain a copy of the booklet *A Consumer Guide To Vehicle Leasing* from the Federal Trade Commission, Regional Office, 8303 Elmbrook Drive, Dallas, TX 75247, telephone (214) 767-7050. This publication, prepared by the FTC in cooperation with the AAA Auto Club Leasing Company and the Automobile Club of Michigan, explains various kinds of leases, advantages and disadvantages of leasing, rights and obligations under leases, and other pertinent items.

BUYING A USED CAR

Purchase of a used car in *good condition,* instead of a new car, is one way of saving money. Getting the best price on that purchase is another way. Avoiding some of the traps and scams mentioned earlier, such as paying too much for a service contract or financing, is yet a third.

There are several sources for used vehicles: private individuals, new car dealers, used car dealers, estate sales, rental car agencies, car leasing companies, or government auctions (see Chapter 17 *Auctions* and Chapter 22 *U. S. Government Property).* And, sometimes corporations will sell their used cars to employees at replacement time, rather than trading them in.

Check It Out: Note that *good condition* and *best possible price* are the operative phrases in buying a used vehicle. You should check the car out yourself visually for signs of damage, excessive wear on the upholstery and carpets, repainting in certain areas, missing or inoperative accessories, etc. In addition, if you are buying from a dealer, try to get the name and address of the former owner and check with him on the car's condition and prior history. If you are dealing with an individual, ask to see the maintenance and repair records. Test drive the car on streets and on highways or freeways. See how

it feels and handles. Listen for any unusual noises. Check all
the accessories to make sure they work.

Finally, have the car checked out by your own mechanic (or
one recommended by a friend or your auto club, if you don't
know one). To do this, you will have to have the permission of
the seller. If he refuses this permission, walk away. He must
have a reason.

Warranties and Service Contracts: Also check out the
warranty situation.   Still valid factory or extended warranties,
or even service contracts, can be transferred to the new owner
in some cases. If you are buying the car from a dealer, the
Federal Trade Commission's Used Car Rule requires the dealer
to place a "Buyer's Guide" sticker in the car window. This
sticker must state whether the car is being sold in "as is"
condition or whether there is a warranty, either specific or
implied. If there is a warranty, find out *exactly* what is covered,
and request that it be put in writing. Private sellers are not
covered by this rule.

For more detailed information on this subject, write and ask
for a copy of the FTC fact sheets on "Warranties" and "Service
Contracts" from: Public Reference, Federal Trade Commission,
Washington, D.C. 20580.

Price Information: To determine the general price levels for
various car makes and models, you can check the ads in your
local newspaper and car trading tabloids. Also check the ads run
by individuals in your newspaper and local throw-away shopping
papers for cars with the specifications you are looking for.
Remember two things: (l) dealer ads may well be "come on"
ads which may or may not be available when you show up at the
lot; (2), even if the ads are genuine, the prices quoted are the
dealer's asking prices. You should be able to negotiate a lower
price than that—in many cases, much lower!

If you are a member of an auto club (such as AAA), it should
be able to provide some pricing information. In addition, the

AAA has available to its members booklets containing tips on buying either used or new cars.

Some of the services mentioned above under new cars also offer pricing guidelines on used vehicles. The one which is probably most widely used is the Kelley Blue Book (in this case, for used cars) which is available at many public libraries. The figures quoted in these books, however, are averages which may not apply in your area or to your situation. You will be much better off by determining the local price level yourself.

TRADE-INS

If you have a car which you were planning to trade in, whether on a new car or another used car, you should strongly consider selling it yourself. You will come out ahead, because the best price you can hope for from the dealer is wholesale price (if you're a good bargainer and know the value of your car), whereas with a little patience you could sell it at or near the going retail price to an individual.

Determining the Price: To determine the general retail price level for your car, follow the same method outlined in this chapter in connection with *shopping* for a used car. To determine the *specific* value of *your* vehicle, take it to at least three used car lots, tell them you are interested in selling your car if you can get enough for it, and ask them to bid on it. You should have first washed and cleaned your auto and had any necessary repairs done. Otherwise you won't be offered top dollar.

FINANCING

As mentioned earlier, if you don't intend to pay cash for a vehicle, whether new or used, you should shop around for financing before you start shopping for the car. Go to a couple of banks, your savings & loan, and (if you belong to one) your credit union. Have each of them put their offer in writing, including the period of time they will hold it open.

If you request a financing offer from a dealer, also have him put his offer in writing, but keep the negotiations on this separate from those on the car itself. Otherwise, you are giving the salesman an opportunity to jack you around on both the car price *and* the financing charge. Before discussing financing with a dealer, we suggest you write to the Bureau of Consumer Protection, Federal Trade Commission, Washington, DC 20580 for a copy of the free brochure *Car Ads: Low Interest Loans & Other Offers.*

For each offer, have the potential lender spell out (1) the principal amount of the loan, (2) the amount of the monthly payment, and (3) the number of payments. By multiplying (2) times (3) and subtracting (1) from the total, you can determine what you would actual pay in finance charges in each case.

Some dealers (and financial, institutions for that matter) may be remiss in explaining their interpretation of "interest rate" or "finance charge." This is an area that some unscrupulous dealers use to increase the total price paid by buyers.

ADDITIONAL INFORMATION SOURCES

Consumer Reports publishes books containing ratings and other useful information on both new and used autos, entitled *Used Car Buying Guide*, and *New Car Buying Guide*. Your local library may have current editions of these on hand. If not, they may be ordered from **Consumer Reports Books**, 9180 Le Saint Drive, Fairfield, OH 45014-9905 for $8.95 each plus $3.00 each shipping and handling.

Chapter 9

AUTO RENTALS

The car rental industry has managed to gain a reputation for itself almost as unsavory as that attaching to used car dealers — deservedly so, unfortunately. This has been brought about by a number of practices, many of which fall under the heading of "incomplete disclosure" (a better term might be "false advertising").

HIDDEN COSTS

Costs with which many rental companies hit their unsuspecting clients include charges for: fuel, airport surcharge, excess mileage, additional driver charges, drop-off or pickup fees, unwanted insurance, infant seats, emergency road services, and taxes. Some operators have been more flagrant than others in failing to inform their customers that certain fees would apply, or in sticking them with unwarranted charges.

The *Los Angeles Times* reported in April 1989 that Alamo Rent A Car was going to change the way it charged customers for fuel refilling. According to the report, Alamo (and some other rental agencies) had been making a mandatory fuel charge, regardless of how much gas was in a car's tank when it was returned. The Federal Trade Commission had filed a lawsuit against Alamo alleging that the company failed to disclose the mandatory gasoline fee or its airport access surcharges when giving price quotes. Alamo agreed to a consent order in the matter, according to the report.

OVERCHARGING FOR REPAIRS

Even Hertz, probably the best-known car rental company of them all, has participated in shenanigans which have been all to typical. According to an article in *Consumer Reports* (July

1989), Hertz admitted to having not only overcharged customers and insurance companies for repairs, but had billed for work never done, falsified repair bills, and forged appraisers' estimate forms. Hertz' tab for the foregoing, according to the article, was a $6.8 million fine and an agreement to make restitution of $13.7 million, as a result of a plea bargain with the federal Government. In a civil settlement with 41 state Attorneys General, Hertz was to pay another $2.3 million in restitution.

PROTECT YOURSELF

Governments at various levels are endeavoring to force the rental companies to clean up their acts. In the meantime, it is up to the individual renter to protect himself while at the same time striving to get the best rental deal available. As stressed throughout this report, it is a matter of collecting and comparing appropriate market information.

Before reserving a rental car, make up a simple worksheet listing the following items down the left side of the sheet. Then check with a number of rental companies (at least three or four, using their 800 number if they have one) to obtain the data. Items to be listed: Car size or type, rental period, basic rate, mileage cap, charge per mile over cap, fuel charges, CDW insurance, other insurance, airport surcharge, taxes, age requirement, credit card requirement, deposit requirement, and (if applicable) drop-off or pickup, and additional driver charges.

You should include at least one or two of the lower tier rental companies such as American International, Enterprise or Thrifty in your survey. Their rates are usually (but not always) lower than the larger, more widely advertised companies. And, if you are *really* serious about saving money, contact Ugly Duckling, Rent-A-Wreck or similar used-car rental agencies. Some of these are strictly local, but Ugly Duckling and Rent-A-Wreck locations now number in the hundreds. If you just want transportation and are not trying to impress someone, you can save up to 50% with one of these alternatives.

AVOID INSURANCE YOU DON'T NEED

Rental agencies try to sell insurance for various types of coverage on all rentals. You should first determine whether your own auto insurance policy covers you when driving a rental car (the majority of them do). If not, and you plan to pay rental charges with a credit card, check with the credit card company. Some of them offer free collision coverage to their customers in an effort to boost their own business.

Refuse other coverage which the rental companies try to flog to you unless your particular circumstances necessitates the coverage. You will probably already be covered for most of them under your auto, homeowner's, personal liability, or AD&D policies.

INSPECT THE VEHICLE

Before driving away in a rented car, check all around for any visible damages—no matter how slight. Make a note on the rental contract of any you find and have the rental agent initial your notation. Also, check to make sure the fuel tank is full. If it is not, have it filled before you leave the rental lot.

CHECK THE BILL

Unless you are rushed for time, take your rental contract to the counter and let the attendant calculate total charges when you turn the car in, rather than using the "express" check-in system. Look the figures over carefully to make sure they are correct. An error is usually more apt to be caught here than later, and much easier to correct than trying to do it by telephone or mail days or weeks later.

Chapter 10

AUTOMOBILE OPERATING COSTS

Major vehicle operating costs are (1) fuel, (2) maintenance & repairs, and (3) insurance. The first two of these categories are covered in this chapter. Insurance was covered in Chapter 6 with other types of insurance.

FUEL AND OIL

Fuel costs are a major expense. They are becoming more so with recent federal and state increases in fuel taxes. The recent Middle East situation has seen a yo-yo effect on prices, but the long term outlook is for continued price increases—probably to new heights. While these increases are beyond the motorist's control, it is possible to keep fuel costs to a minimum with a little effort.

Don't fall for oil company ads touting premium fuels unless your car is equipped with a high-performance engine which requires it. Ninety percent of today's autos run perfectly well on regular unleaded gasoline. You can determine the grade of fuel required for your car by checking the octane number specified in your owner's manual.

If you buy premium gasoline when all you really need is regular, you are throwing your money away. At a price difference of up to twenty cents (more, in some cases), you could save over $100 per year by using non-premium if your average use is ten gallons per week.

SERVE YOURSELF AND PAY CASH

The difference between self-serve and full-service prices is substantial. A recent survey of gasoline stations (most of them no longer deserve the name "service stations") in the author's neighborhood revealed price differences ranging from 12 cents to 46 cents per gallon between self-serve and full-service. The 10-gallon per week user would save from $62 to $239 per year by pumping his own gas. (This survey also turned up the ridiculous fact that some stations charge different prices per gallon for pumping various grades of fuel, as if it were more work or required more time to pump premium than regular!).

Another price differential at some stations was based on the use of a credit card versus paying cash. This spread varied from four to six cents per gallon.

SHOP AROUND

The final price spread to watch out for is the one between different gasoline stations for the same class fuel. The above mentioned survey, which covered seven stations, found maximum spreads of 7.4% on regular leaded, 17% on regular unleaded, 16% on low premium unleaded, 16% on medium premium unleaded, 7.5% on high premium unleaded, and 20% on diesel #2. Oil companies included Chevron, Mobil, Shell (2), Texaco, and Unocal (2). One interesting finding was that the biggest price differential of all between stations (20%) was between two stations selling the same oil company's product!

STRETCH YOUR MILEAGE

Saving on price is only part of the story in saving on fuel costs. Equally important is to reduce fuel usage by getting as many miles per gallon as possible. It is possible to reduce consumption by up to 20 percent by following a few rules and tips which are contained in a free booklet available from the American Automobile Association. Write to *AAA Gas Watcher's Guide*, Mail Stop 150, 1000 AAA Drive, Heathrow, FL 32746-5063, and enclose a stamped self-addressed #10 envelope. Members may pick up a copy at their local AAA office.

Summary: To sum up, for greatest fuel savings use fuel with the proper octane rating, pump your own gas, pay cash (if the cash price is lower) and, most important, compare prices at several gasoline stations in your area. This comparison should be done frequently.

MAINTENANCE AND REPAIR

Repairs will be fewer and less costly if the service and maintenance procedures and schedules called out in the car owner's manual are rigorously followed. Even so, there will come a time when repairs of some type will become necessary.

Check Your Warranty and Service Policies: If your car is relatively new, first determine whether the problem is covered by warranty. You should be able to determine this by referring to the owner's manual. If you're not sure, call a dealer and ask him; if the dealer says no or appears to be unsure, ask for the telephone number of the regional office of the automobile's *manufacturer*, then check with that office. When a large number of cars of a particular model develop the same problem, manufacturers sometimes take it upon themselves to absorb the repair cost for reasons of customer relations.

If you have purchased a service policy and your problem is not covered by manufacturer's warranty, it may be covered by the service policy. This can be determined by referring to terms of the policy.

Independent Repair Shops: Except for repairs covered by warranties or service policies which usually (but not always) require repairs to be carried out by a dealer, you should have a reliable independent garage lined up that you can call upon. The rates charged by most independents are less than dealerships, and there is the further advantage of getting to personally know the owner and mechanics who will be doing your work. Using an independent in whom you have confidence and with whom you have developed a trusting relationship will not only save money on repairs actually done, but will give you confidence that only *necessary* work is performed.

If you don't already have a repair shop lined up, you could start by asking two or three friends or business associates for their recommendation. Other sources for guidance are your auto club, the local Better Business Bureau, and consumer guides available at your local library. Make up a list of the more promising candidates, then visit each of them and talk to the owner or manager.

Explain that you are considering the shop for future work, and you want to meet the management and look over the facilities. Ask how long the shop has been in business, and about the experience of the mechanics. You could also ask for the names and phone numbers of some current customers to check for references.

Look over the premises to see if they are clean and orderly. Decide whether the atmosphere is friendly but business-like. See if the establishment displays a sign signifying approval by a major auto club, and/or certification by the National Institute of Automotive Service Excellence (ASE). The auto club approval will apply to the establishment, the ASE certifications to individual mechanics.

Get An Estimate: Finally, whether you use a dealership, an independent, or a national chain, always ask for a written estimate before authorizing any repair work. Make sure you understand what work is being quoted and why it is necessary before authorizing the job.

Chapter 11

AIRLINE FARES

For anyone unfamiliar with the complexities of air fares, obtaining the best price on an airline ticket can prove to be a daunting experience. Not only do the airlines have different classes of service, most of them have several sub-divisions within these categories. In addition, they frequently run promotion specials which may apply to certain destinations only, or which are limited to a given time period. They also have special deals that are not advertised and are little-known, even to travel agents.

Getting the lowest priced fare available should be as simple as picking up the telephone and calling a travel agent or airline, but it doesn't work out that way. The New York City Department of Consumer Affairs did an exercise in the summer of 1990 in which they called more than four dozen travel agencies and requested the lowest advance purchase fares possible between New York and a handful of destinations. Prices quoted by the agencies varied up to 50% in some cases! Lesson: Always compare prices quoted by at least two or three travel agents, and the same number of airlines.

Almost all of the major airlines have special rates for tickets purchased a specified number of days in advance of a trip. Always inquire whether B, H, K, L, M, Q or V fares are available—these are designations for lower priced economy or discounted fares.

Low priced advance purchase tickets are subject to a welter of restrictions which affect pricing and which—if violated—can result in very significant penalties. To avoid this undesirable result, it is important that the ticket buyer ask his travel agent (or airline if purchased direct) for a full explanation of *all* requirements and restrictions.

Several airlines have special discount programs which are available to groups such as military personnel or senior citizens. Some of them also have ticket *coupon* books for senior citizens which offer substantial savings, even when compared to other discount programs.   Airlines offering these senior specials are listed in Chapter 25 *Special Deals for Senior Citizens.*

To make matters even more confusing for international flights, there are operators (known as Consolidators) which buy cut-rate tickets in large packages and make them available to the public at special low prices.   Then there are tour operators which include the cost of the airline ticket in a package which might include hotels, some meals, ground transportation, etc., making it impossible to identify the cost of the air fare.

Finally, there are the charter airlines which may or may not offer a lower price, or better service, or both.   The major charter operators from the U. S. are shown later in this chapter.

ADVANCE TICKET PURCHASE

It helps to get a low priced fare if you can be flexible in your travel plans.   Flexibility will allow you to take advantage of super saver fares offered by most major airlines under ATP plans.   Advance purchase usually means you must make your reservations from 14 to 30 days in advance, that you can fly on certain days of the week only, and that you must stay over at least one Saturday night.   Each airline sets aside a limited number of low fare seats on each flight, so the earlier you make your reservation, the better chance you will have.   Requirements and restrictions vary from one airline to another, so be sure and request full details when calling.

APEX INTERNATIONAL FARES

APEX (advance purchase excursion) fares are the international equivalent of domestic ATP's.   APEX fares can save the traveler up to 40% off published full-price fares.   As with ATP's, certain restrictions apply—usually relating to length of journey. Request full details before booking.

BE READY

Whether for a domestic or international flight, when you have determined the lowest price available and have decided that you can accept whatever restrictions apply, be prepared to commit for your reservation and ticket purchase right then before the price changes or the low-priced seats are sold out.

SENIOR SPECIALS

As mentioned above, for special discounts and low-priced coupon flight books offered to senior citizens by several major airlines, refer to Chapter 25.

CONSOLIDATORS

In the travel section of Sunday editions of major newspapers, you will find cut-rate airline tickets advertised by consolidators (formerly called "bucket shops"). These are firms that sell mostly international tickets, although a few are starting to handle some domestic flights, which the airlines have sold to the consolidator at a discount. Part of this discount is passed on to the traveler.

It is often possible to save money buying from a consolidator. It is also possible to pay more than you would if you had shopped around at other sources. Prices vary from one consolidator to another, and from season to season. Purchasers should also bear in mind that consolidator tickets carry higher risks than regular tickets. For example, refunds are not always available if your plans change, you cannot change airlines should you decide to do so, getting a confirmed seat can sometimes be a problem, your credit card might not be accepted for payment, and there may be undisclosed restrictions.

As with any other major purchase, shop around before committing to a consolidator. Compare prices between consolidators, and with APEX, tour operators, charters, and even published regular fares. Evaluate not only the fares but all applicable restrictions and regulations.

A good place to begin in checking out consolidators would be to contact **British European Travel, 3707 Williams Rd, Suite 100, San Jose, CA 95117, telephone (408) 984-5480.** This organization sells discounted tickets—coach, business and first class—within the U.S. as well as to and from Europe.

Information on other consolidators can be obtained through travel agencies (agencies can buy from consolidators), from the travel section of newspapers, or from one of the travel advisor publications listed later in this chapter.

CHARTER AIRLINES

Travelers planning a trip to Europe should not overlook charter airlines. The following companies operate modern, well-appointed aircraft and have established good reputations in this field. Their points of departure and destinations are limited, but if you live near one of their take-off points it could be to your advantage to check out their schedules and fares. Charter bookings are normally handled by tour operators, but can be done by travel agents or—in some cases—directly with the airline. Call the numbers shown for specific information.

Balair LTD, Swiss Center, 8th Floor, 608 Fifth Avenue, New York, NY 10020. Tel. (800) 221-4750 or (212) 581-3411. This partially-owned subsidiary of Swissair has flights from New York, Bangor, Miami, Los Angeles and San Francisco to Switzerland.

Condor, John Hancock Center, Suite 3222, 875 N. Michigan Avenue, Chicago, IL 60611. Tel. (800) 782-2424 or (312) 951-0005. Condor is a Lufthansa subsidiary which flies to Frankfurt,

Germany from Chicago, Denver, Los Angeles, New York, Cleveland, San Francisco, Fort Lauderdale and Tampa.

LTU International Airways, 6033 West Century Blvd., Suite 1000 Los Angeles, CA 90045-6419. Tel. (800) 888-0200 or (213) 337-7514. LTU is an independent airline with flights from New York, Miami, Los Angeles, San Francisco and Honolulu to points in Germany.

Martinair Holland, 1165 Northern Boulevard, Manhasset, NY 11030. Tel. (800) 847-6677 or (516) 627-8711. Martinair is partly owned by KLM Royal Dutch Airlines. It operates flights to Amsterdam from Baltimore/Washington, Detroit, Los Angeles, Miami, Minneapolis, Newark, New York, San Francisco, Seattle, Tampa, Toronto and Puerto Plata (Dom. Rep.).

Note: Departure points and destinations of charter airlines are subject to change, and are normally fewer in off-season. Check with the airline for current information.

AN ALTERNATIVE

One airline which does not fit the Charter description but which normally offers cross-Atlantic flights at substantially lower fares than the major airlines is **Virgin Atlantic**. If you are departing from either the East Coast or West Coast of the USA for London, include this line when making price comparisons.

THE PC CONNECTION

If you have a personal computer equipped with a modem and subscribe to CompuServe, GEnie, Prodigy or one of the other PC networks tied in to an airline information and reservation system such as **OAG** (the clearing house for all airlines), or **American Airline's Eaasy Sabre,** you can run your own search for the lowest *published* air fare. You can also make reservations and purchase tickets via computer if you wish.

If you then would like an additional savings to compensate yourself for acting as your own travel agent, you can take the flight and fare information you have developed and contact one of the following discount travel agents. These agents charge a minimum fee for processing airline tickets and rebate the difference between that fee and their commission to the buyer. A telephone call to one or more of the agencies listed below will provide more detailed information on the subject.

DISCOUNT TRAVEL AGENTS

Travel Avenue, 641 W. Lake Street,   Chicago, IL 60606. Tel (800) 333-3335.

Pennsylvania Travel, 19 E. Central Avenue, Paoli, PA 19301. Tel. (800) 331-0947 or (215) 251-9944.

The $mart Traveler, 3111 SW 27th Avenue, Miami, FL 33133. Tel. (800) 226-3338 or (305) 448-3338.

TRAVEL ADVISORS

For the person who takes more than an occasional trip, or who is planning a long trip or foreign vacation, a subscription to one of several travel publications could prove to be a good investment. These cover not only the latest developments on air fares, but include much other information useful to the traveler. We suggest that you contact two or more of the following and request that descriptive material be sent to you so you can determine which one would fit your particular needs. (If you are not a frequent traveler, check your local library and see if they subscribe to one of these travel publications).

Some travel advisory publications also offer an airline reservation and ticket buying service under which they guarantee the lowest available price. Bear in mind that the guarantee may refer to the lowest officially published price—not necessarily the lowest price obtainable from sources other than the airline.

Following is a representative list of Travel Advisors:

Best Fares, Box 17212, Arlington, TX 76003, Tel. (800) 635-3033, $68.00 per year (monthly).

Consumer Reports Travel Letter, Box 53629, Boulder, CO 80322-3629.   Tel. (800) 999-7959.   Price $37.00 per year (monthly).

ITN International Travel News, 1779 Tribute Rd, Suite L, Sacramento, CA 95815.   Price $14.00 per year (monthly).

Stand-Buys, Operations Center, P. O. Box 1017, Trumbull, CT 06611-9934.   Tel. (800) 255-0200.   Price $49.00 per year (monthly).

Travel Smart, Communications House, Inc., Dobbs Ferry, NY 10522.   Tel. (800) 327-3633.   Price $37.00 per year (monthly).

OTHER TRAVEL TIPS

The importance of schedule flexibility in obtaining low-priced advance ticket purchases was emphasized earlier in this chapter. This also applies to catching special seasonal promotions laid on by the airlines. As an example, fares from the U. S. to Europe are usually lower between November and May than during the rest of the year.

Unexpected events can cause special promotions by airlines. Air carriers tool up to carry a given number of passengers on each route, based on experience and forecasts. When expected traffic doesn't materialize, they end up with a too many unsold seats.   As any other business would do, they then conduct a "sale" in the form of reduced prices over specified routes for a given time period. Their competitors on those routes, to protect their own markets, almost invariably meet (or beat) the new prices. Hence, travelers who can wait to take a trip, and are patient, can often end up with a much lower fare.

Always Ask: Seasonal and other special promotions are usually advertised in major newspapers by the airlines running them, but not always. Therefore, when talking to an airline or travel agent it pays to **always** ask about any special fares they are offering at the moment—in fact, it often pays to ask two or three airlines and travel agencies. As mentioned earlier in this chapter, there are times when the person you are talking to is uninformed about the latest fares—or just doesn't bother to tell you.

If you are a subscriber to one of the travel advisors listed above, give them a ring for the latest fare information. They are usually on top of things.

PRICING QUIRKS

Due to anomalies in pricing structures, it is sometimes possible to find a fare to a destination *past* the point to which you want to travel that is lower than the fare to your intended destination. In other words, the fare for a trip from A to C via B is actually cheaper than a trip from A to B. These are sometimes referred to as hidden city fares. The traveler could save money by buying a round-trip ticket A to C, even though his destination is B.

According to an article which appeared in *Investor's Daily*, a study by the Boeing Co. showed that at 18 "hub" airports where a single airline has 50% of the traffic, travelers flying through the hub on connecting flights paid as much as 30% below average fares, while those whose trip began or ended at the hubs paid 40% to 50% more.

Unfortunately, most airlines frown on someone taking advantage of their fare-setting goofs, and if they find out about it during your trip (which they will, if you don't board the return flight at C), may cancel your reservation or force you to ante up additional fare money. Note that they can do this only on round-trip flights, so it is much safer to use this on one way flights only. To beat the round-trip problem, you could book two one-way flights. The publication *Best Fares* mentioned above under travel advisors publishes lists of hidden-city fares.

A somewhat similar situation—and one the airlines cannot object to the traveler exploiting—is where the fare from A to C is higher than the sum of the fares from A to B and B to C. In this case the traveler going to C buys two tickets (roundtrip or one-way); one from A to B and the other from B to C.

You probably won't be successful in getting a travel agent to search out the foregoing special situations because of the time involved. If you are a PC user who subscribes to CompuServe, GEnie or Prodigy, you could have a go at it on your own.

PASSENGER RIGHTS

For additional practical advice on airline travel, including what to do about lost tickets, missing baggage, and canceled or overbooked flights, order the booklet *Fly-Rights: A Guide to Air Travel in the U.S.*, from Consumer Information Center-K, P. O. Box 100, Pueblo, CO 81002. Enclose a check or money order for $1.00 with you order. This pamphlet was prepared by the U. S. Department of Transportation.

Chapter 12

HOTELS AND MOTELS

Whether on a business trip or on vacation, hotel or motel costs are a major part of the traveler's expenses. To the uninformed, these costs are usually higher than they need to be. All hostelries have a room price list (referred to as the "rack rate"). This is what they quote if you just ask about rates. But, as with most other products and services, supply and demand usually determine the selling price. The knowledgeable traveler can take advantage of this fact.

Hotel employees will not go out of their way to inform inquirers about lower rates, especially if they think they can sell the room at full price. It is up to you to shop, compare and negotiate just as if you were buying any other commodity. This chapter will provide information to help you do this effectively.

WHAT DO YOU WANT?

The starting place in planning travel savings is to determine what you want in the way of accommodations. Many people make the mistake of booking space at plush hotels which offer spas, indoor swimming pools, exercise rooms, convention facilities, and other amenities when all they really want is a comfortable place to spend the night. If a bed for the night is all you are looking for, you can find plenty of them at bargain prices.

If, on the other hand, you do want to stay at a posh place it is possible to obtain substantial discounts at these as well. Even with a good discount most of these places will still be more expensive than economy chains where you can get clean, comfortable and convenient quarters at a low price—and often qualify for a discount as well. Some of the motels that fit this category are **Comfort Inn, Days Inn, Econo Lodge, Hampton Inns, La Quinta (which allows pets), Motel 6, Red Roof, and Rodeway Inns.**

WHEN TO TRAVEL

Since supply and demand affect price, travel when room demand will be low if you have the flexibility to do so. For example, winter is generally better than other seasons and even autumn and spring are better than summer. Unless you specifically want to attend them, avoid traveling to any destination during special occasions such as festivals, major sporting events, autumn foliage tours, large conventions, etc. If you are not sure whether there might be a conflict, call the Chamber of Commerce in the area where you plan to travel.

If you have the flexibility, holidays and weekends are good times to visit larger cities where hotels and motels do much of their business during the week with business travelers. Many of them offer reduced weekend and holiday rates which are available to anyone *who asks*. It's up to you to inquire about these specials. When you are quoted a rate, ask "is that the best price you have?" Sometimes you will be offered a further concession in the form of an even lower price, a later check-out time, free breakfast, or some other goody.

MEMBERSHIP DISCOUNTS

If you are a member of the American Association of Retired Persons (AARP), the American Automobile Association (AAA), the International Airline Passengers Association (IAPA), the military, a government employee, a travel club, or are a teacher or other employee in the field of education, you can obtain a discount at many hotels and motels. Whenever enquiring about reservations and rates, inform the hotel of your membership affiliation and inquire whether you qualify for a special rate.

Should your hotel stay be in connection with a trade show or convention which you are attending, your group has probably negotiated a special group rate for attendees. When making your reservation, mention your affiliation and make sure you are receiving this rate.

TRAVEL CLUBS

The average occupancy rate at hotels and motels nationwide in the U.S. in recent months has been estimated at less than 65%. It is even lower in some sections of the country. A hotel room is an extremely perishable commodity. If it is not sold, the revenue for that night is lost forever. It makes economic sense for the hotel to sell the room at almost any price rather than have it remain empty. Even if it is sold at cost, the hotel's overhead is covered and the guest may spend some money in the hotel restaurant or gift shop.

This economic fact of life is the driving force behind travel clubs which offer hotel and motel discounts of up to 50% to members. Annual club membership fees run from $30 to $100, so a club membership doesn't make sense for someone who plans to be on the road only two or three nights per year. If you travel more than this, these "half-price" discount clubs offer a real savings opportunity.

There are a number of considerations to take into account before signing up for one of these programs. Although several of the major hotel chains participate in one or more club listings, not all of their locations are included. All discounted rooms are subject to availability. What that means is that if the hotel thinks it can sell the room at full price, it won't be available under a discount program. And, when available, these deep discounts apply to the full published (rack) rate for the room—they cannot be used in conjunction with other discounts or promotions.

Some of the participating hotels include only their higher priced rooms in these programs, which means you might be better off with a smaller discount (or none at all) at some other place. Other restrictions such as length of stay or seasonal availability, may apply as well. These will vary from one hotel to another.

The hotels listed with each travel club will vary, as will membership fees and services offered by the club. Listed below is a selection of clubs from several which are available. Space does not permit the inclusion of every travel club which exists, but we consider this list to be a representative cross-section with which you can begin your investigation and evaluation of the programs available to the traveler. The names and addresses of other clubs can be found in some of the travel advisory publications listed in Chapter 11 *Airline Fares*.

Please note that members of most of these clubs may receive other benefits such as airline and rental car discounts, special prices on tours and cruises, newsletters, travel insurance, etc. Therefore, it pays to request information from several of them and compare *all relevant data* before making a selection. You should examine each club in light of your own travel requirements *before* signing up with any of them.

Concierge, 1050 Yuma St, Suite 310, Denver, CO 80204. Tel. (800) 346-1022. Annual membership $69.95. Offers 50% discounts on more than 450 U. S. and international hotels and motels. Members receive directory of participating hotels and motels. Concierge claims a confirmation rate of about 95% of all member requests, which is extremely high for this type of program.

CUC Travel Services, Inc., P. O. Box 1016, Trumbull, CT 06611-1016. Tel. (800) 248-4234. This is another discount program offered by the ubiquitous CUC International (mentioned elsewhere in this volume). The program is available from **CUC (Travelers Advantage), Citibank (CitiTravel), and Sears (Sears Discount Travel Club).** Check with the one of your choice for membership costs. Offers 50% discounts at nearly 1300 hotels and motels. Members receive discount hotel directory.

Discount Travel International, The Ives Building, Suite 205, Narberth, PA 19072. Tel. (215) 668-7184. Annual membership $45.00. (Members of the **Prodigy** personal computer network get a special price of $29.95). Members are automatically enrolled in **The Buying Network**, a computerized discount shopping service. Program includes discounts on air fares, tours, and cruises in addition to 50% discount at over 900 hotels and motels in the United States and Canada.

Encore, 4501 Forbes Blvd, Lanham, MD 20706. Tel. (800) 638-0930. Annual membership $48.00. Offers 50% discounts at more than 2400 hotels, motels and resorts. Directory provided to members.

Quest International Corporation, Chinook Tower, Box 4041, Yakima, WA 98901. Tel. (800) 325-2400. Annual membership $99.00. Offers 50% discount at nearly 1600 participating hotels in the US, Canada, Caribbean, Mexico and Europe. Hotel directory provided. Memberships available directly from **Quest** at above address, through many associations, clubs, and organizations, and via **Prodigy** personal computer network.

Travelers Plus/World Unlimited, 6404 Nancy Ridge Drive, San Diego, CA 92121-2248. Tel. (outside CA) (800) 237-0952, (CA) (800) 843-0265. Annual membership $39.95. Offers 50% discounts at over 2000 hotel, motel and resort locations. Directory provided to members.

OTHER POSSIBILITIES

If you don't travel enough to justify membership in a travel club and are not a member of one of the organizations mentioned earlier, you can probably still obtain a hotel or motel room below the "rack" rate. Armed with the information in this report you can attempt to negotiate your own special rate. If that doesn't work, or you don't want to be bothered, many travel agencies have arrangements under which they obtain hotel discounts from companies which book blocks of rooms with certain hotels or chains.

If you're planning a trip, ask a local travel agent if it has such an arrangement. If not, you can call **THOR24** at (303) 449-2049 and ask for the name of a travel agent in your area that subscribes to their service. **THOR24** has a portfolio consisting of approximately 12,000 corporate rates, 685 preferred rates, and over 600 special corporate rates which they offer only through member travel agencies. Discounts available will be less than the "half-price" rates offered by travel clubs, but any discount is better than none. Room availability will probably not be as restricted under these block arrangements as they are under the half-price programs.

Chapter 13

COMPUTERS AND ACCESSORIES

The marketing strategy for suppliers of personal computers and computer-related products has very quickly and rather quietly undergone a major revolution. The computer supermarket, computer showrooms, and mail-order houses have arrived on the scene, bringing with them major price savings for the consumer on just about everything in the computer world. Everyday prices at these retailers range from 30% to 80% below "normal" resale!

A related companion to this phenomenon is the explosive growth of office products superstores, which are covered in a later chapter. Indeed, there is a certain amount of overlap in the two markets, so when shopping for computer accessories or supplies don't overlook the suppliers listed in the office supply section, and *vice versa.*

COMPUTERS

The term "computer" as used in this book means a personal computer set-up consisting of a central processing unit (CPU), a keyboard, a monitor, and a printer. These are the units required to make up a basic operating system. Other hardware, such as a modem, a mouse, etc. are considered accessories or peripherals.

WHAT SHOULD YOU BUY?

The most important point to remember in shopping for a computer is to buy the equipment that fits your needs. Buying more computer than you will need in the foreseeable future is a waste of money. Equally wasteful is not buying enough in the form of capacity, speed or features to adequately handle your requirements. This can be costly in inconvenience and lost time, or in having to upgrade or replace the equipment.

If you are a beginner in the PC field, or even a somewhat experienced user who is not sure what he should buy, we suggest you read articles or books on the subject available at your local library such as *Personal Computer Buying Guide*, Consumer Reports Books, 9180 Le Saint Drive, Fairfield, OH 45014-9905 (tel. 513-860-1178); $10.95 plus #3.00 s&h; or *The Secret Guide to Computers,* by Russ Walter (author & publisher), 22 Ashland St, Somerville, MA 02144; three volumes in one, $15.00.

Either of the above books may be ordered directly from the publisher if your library doesn't have a copy. The U. S. Government Printing Office has a low-priced alternative entitled *How to Buy A Personal Computer*, (priced at only $0.50), available from Consumer Information Center, P. O. Box 100, Pueblo, CO 81102. It is not as comprehensive as the other publications, but may very well serve your purpose.

WHERE YOU CAN BUY IT

When you are confident enough to begin shopping for your PC equipment, below are a few suppliers which offer substantial savings:

CompuAdd, 12303 Technology Blvd, Austin, TX 78727, telephone (800) 627-1967. Computers, accessories, and software. In addition to their mail order business, CompuAdd operates 90 stores nationwide and has plans to add 60 or so more. CompuAdd offers a 30-day money-back guarantee on hardware products, and a limited one-year warranty on all products. Mail orders or telephone orders are accepted at the address or 800 number given above. Call the 800 number for a catalog and to get the address and telephone number of the store nearest you.

CompUSA (formerly Soft Warehouse), 15160 Marsh Lane, Dallas, TX 75234, telephone (800) 451-7638. Computers, accessories, furniture, and software. This computer superstore has over 5000 products to choose from, and its aggressive pricing policy offers savings of 30% to 80% off standard retail. Their catalog may be ordered by calling the 800 number listed above. CompUSA operates superstores in **California, Colorado, Georgia, Illinois, Michigan, Pennsylvania, Texas, and Virginia.** Their catalog lists the street address, telephone number, and (where applicable) FAX number for each of their locations. This company has an aggressive expansion plan, so if your town isn't listed above give them a call at the 800 number anyway. There may be one on the way to your area.

Computer Direct, 22292 N. Pepper Rd, Barrington, IL 60010, telephone (800) 289-9473. Computers, accessories, software and supplies. This mail-order only operation (unless you live in the Chicago area) operates under the motto "We Love Our Customers!" They offer a 15-day home trial and a 90-day replacement period, and state that they will match any current valid nationally advertised price. Savings of up to 70% on some items are advertised. Orders accepted by FAX (708-382-7545), computer on-line (708-382-3270), or telephone. Call the 800 number shown above for a catalog.

Corporate Express, 13800 East 39th Ave, Aurora, CO 80011-1608, telephone (800) 735-8700 (outside CO), or (303) 373-8444 (in CO), FAX (303) 373-7629. Computers, accessories, software, and office machines. This highly successful operation was started from the home of its founders in 1984 as a computerized on-line supplier of software. It has since expanded its line to include several brands and models of PC's plus accessory and peripheral equipment. The 300-plus page catalog of Corporate Express may be ordered by calling one of the numbers shown above. Orders may be placed by phone or FAX as listed, or by computer modem via CompuServe, Delphi, GEnie, Prodigy, or The Source.

COMMENT

As this report is being written, the major computer manufacturers—IBM, Compaq, and Apple—have reduced prices on their lower end models, putting pricing pressure on the vendors listed above, and on "second tier" firms such as AST Research Inc. and Advanced Logic Research, as well as on independent local shops which assemble CPU's from purchased components. As a result of this situation, prices are soft and bargains are available for the shrewd shopper.

As stressed throughout this report, always obtain at least three quotations on major purchases. Compare not only prices and specifications but other terms as well, including warranties, return privileges, and shipping charges.

ACCESSORIES & SUPPLIES

For computer supplies and desktop accessories at prices lower than manufacturer's suggested retail, check out the following in addition to the sources listed above:

MEI/Micro Center, 1100 Steelwood Road, Columbus, OH 43212, telephone (800) 634-3478. If you live in the vicinity of Columbus, Ohio, you can visit this company's superstore for supplies at the address above. If not, call the 800 number for their mail order catalog. Their prices are excellent.

QUILL, 100 Schelter Rd, Lincolnshire, IL 60069-3621, telephone (708) 434-4800. This mail-order supplier also handles other office products. It is included here as well as in the office supply section because of its good selection of computer supplies. Quill offers a 90-day no-risk guarantee and free delivery on orders over $45.00. Order are processed and shipped from three locations: Call the above number (unfortunately, Quill does not have an 800 number) for a product catalog which gives the addresses, telephone numbers, and FAX numbers for these locations.

SOFTWARE

The following sources offer three very different types of software—proprietary, Public Domain, and Shareware:

Proprietary Software: Discounted name brand software is available from the following two sources, among several. Refer to the popular personal computer magazines for additional sources, or check with suppliers of other computer items listed in this chapter.

Egghead Discount Software, 22011 S. E. 51st, Issaquah, WA 98027, telephone (800) 344-4323. Egghead is a discount retailer of popular name-brand proprietary programs. This was probably the first major chain specializing in software. It also carries some accessories and supplies in its approximately 175 stores. Call the above 800 number to check prices, place an order, request a catalog, or obtain the address of the store nearest you.

Selective Software, 903 Pacific Avenue, Santa Cruz, CA 95060, telephone (800) 423-3556. This organization offers moderately priced alternative software packages to some of the name brands, as well as some unique accessories and learning programs. Call the 800 number above for a catalog.

Shareware And Public Domain Software: Adequate low-priced software for individual and small business users is available as Public Domain and Shareware programs. Public Domain software may be used, copied, or given away without payment of any fee or royalty, except the price charged for providing you with the copied disk.

Shareware is not free.   You may purchase a program (normally at a very low price) and try it. If you decide that you want to use it, you are morally obligated to pay a fee (usually nominal) to its developer, in addition to the price you may have paid to obtain the copied disk.

Information regarding fee payment is normally incorporated in the introduction to the program on the disk. These programs are available from the following sources, among others:

Shareware Express, 27601 Forbes Rd, Suite 37, Laguna Niguel, CA 92677, telephone (800) 346-2842 (or 714/367-0080 inside California), offers a cross section of quality shareware for personal and business use. A catalog is available by calling one of the above numbers.

Software Excitement, P. O. Box 3072, 6475 Crater Lake Highway, Central Point, OR 97502, telephone (800) 444-5457. This company works with independent software developers to acquire powerful and innovative Shareware programs. Contact them at the address or telephone number above for their catalog which features a broad range of disks for your home or office.

The Software Labs, 3767 Overland Ave #112-115, Los Angeles, CA 90034, telephone (800) 359-9998. TSL carries low-priced commercial proprietary programs, ranging from $22.95 to $161.95, which compete with some of the well-known software disks of major companies selling for several times those numbers. It's largest inventory, however, consists of Public-domain Software & Shareware. 5-1/4" disks containing programs in these two categories sell for $3.49 each, 3-1/2" disks for $4.49 each. If 10 or more are ordered, the prices drop to $2.99 and $3.99 respectively.

Other companies which sell Public Domain software and Shareware may be found listed in some of the popular computer magazines found on newsstands.

A non-commercial source of public domain software is the New York Amateur Computer Club, Inc. Disks costs $4.00 each. Information may be obtained by writing the club at P. O. Box 3442 Church Street Station, New York, NY 10008.

PROBLEMS AND A SOLUTION

Two problems connected with Public Domain and Shareware programs are their abundance and their unknown quality. Just sorting through the hundreds of available programs with their abbreviated and often peculiar names to find one that sounds as if it might fit your needs can be a major problem. After you have done this, you still can't tell from the skimpy description provided in most magazines or catalogs whether it has the features you really need or how difficult it is to use.

Fortunately, there is a convenient solution to both these problems in the form of a book entitled *Public-Domain Software & Shareware* (sub-titled *Untapped Resources for The PC User*) by Rusel DeMaria and George R. Fontaine. Look for this at your local library, or you may order it from the publisher shown below.

The authors have done a yeoman job of separating the wheat from the chaff and have come up with dozens of low-priced easily useable programs that cover almost every conceivable need of the average PC user. Each program is described, and the strong points as well as the weak (if any) are detailed.

Some of the applications covered include accounting, databases, desk managers, games, graphics, learning, DOS shells, spreadsheets, utilities, and word processing. In addition, there are chapters providing background information on public domain and shareware, dealing with telecommunications, explaining archives and libraries, and other useful data.

This book may be ordered from: **M&T BOOKS**, 501 Galveston Drive, Redwood City, CA 94063, Tel. (800) 533-4372, or (800) 356-2002 (within CA). Price $19.95 plus $3.50 S&H (plus sales tax for California residents).

OTHER SOURCES

Don't overlook office superstores and warehouse clubs when shopping for supplies or accessories. Many of them carry at least some supplies, and some of them also carry personal computers, accessories and software.

Chapter 14

OFFICE SUPPLIES

Following on the heels of the explosive growth in membership warehouse clubs which deal in a wide range of merchandise, office megastores which concentrate on office supplies and equipment have hit the scene in a big way. These specialty outlets first appeared on the scene about six years ago. Since then their numbers have increased to approximately 400 stores nationwide, with annual sales in excess of one billion dollars.

These super suppliers of stationery and other office goods cater primarily to businesses—large and small—with special appeal to the thousands of home-based operations now extant in the U.S. Most of them, however, also sell to the general public, in some cases at slightly higher prices. Check with the suppliers of your choice regarding their sales policy and pricing terms.

THE CHANGING SCENE

As has been the case with other new marketing concepts, the office megastore industry is undergoing a certain amount of simultaneous consolidation, streamlining and growth. For example, as this is being written HQ Office Supplies Warehouse Inc. has just sold nine stores in Southern California to Staples Inc. HQ plans to merge with its Canadian affiliate, HQ International Inc. This follows the purchase of the 51-store chain of Office Club by Office Depot.

Because the scene is changing rapidly, listings which follow are subject to continuing change. If you have questions about store locations in your area, check your local yellow pages or contact the headquarters office telephone or address shown for the respective companies.

The range of products carried by each marketer varies, but for the most part may be included in the generic description "office supplies and equipment." For that reason, the listings below do not carry product descriptions but only store locations. For detailed information on products available from each, contact the companies of your choice and request a catalog. Most of these suppliers provide mail-order service as well as local outlets.

Arvey Paper & Office Products, 3351 W. Addison, Chicago, IL 60618, telephone (312) 463-6423, or (800) 992-7839 or (800) 654-0012. *Stores:* **Arizona**: Phoenix. **California**: Oakland, Redwood City, Sacramento, San Francisco, San Jose. **Colorado**: Denver. **Florida:** Ft. Lauderdale, Miami, Orlando, Tampa. **Georgia**: Atlanta, Marietta. **Illinois:** Arlington Heights, Atrium, Chicago (3), Downers Grove (2), Franklin Park, Niles. **Indiana:** Indianapolis. **Kentucky:** Louisville. **Minnesota:** Minneapolis. **Missouri:** Kansas City. **Ohio:** Cincinnati, Columbus. **Oregon**: Portland. **Pennsylvania:** Pittsburgh. **Tennessee:** Memphis. **Texas:** Addison, Austin, Dallas, Houston (3), San Antonio (2). **Utah:** S. Salt Lake City. **Washington**: Bellvue, Seattle.

Office America, P. O. Box 11667, Richmond, VA 23230-1667, telephone (804) 273-0900; FAX (804) 270-2973. *Stores:* **Alabama**: Birmingham. **Indiana**: Indianapolis (2). **North Carolina**: Charlotte, Raleigh (2). **Ohio**: Columbus, Dayton, Dublin, Reynoldsburg. **Tennessee**: Memphis. **Virginia**: Richmond (2).

Office Depot, 851 Broken Sound Parkway, N.W., Boca Raton, FL 33487, telephone (407) 994-2131. *Stores:* **Alabama**: Birmingham (2), Hoover, Huntsville, Mobile. **Arkansas:** Little Rock. **Florida**: Altamonte Springs, Boca Raton (2), Boynton Beach, Clearwater (3), Davie, Daytona Beach, Ft. Lauderdale (2), Ft. Myers, Hialeah, Hollywood, Jacksonville (3), Lakeland, Lauderdale Lakes, Margate, Miami (5), North Miami (2), Orlando (3), Pembroke Pines, Pompano Beach, Sarasota, St. Petersburg, Tallahassee, Tampa (3), West Melbourne, West Palm Beach. **Georgia:** Atlanta (3), Augusta, Duluth, Jonesboro, Norcross, Sandy Springs, Smyrna, Stone Mountain.

Indiana: Clarksville, Evansville, Fort Wayne, Indianapolis (4). **Iowa**: West Des Moines. **Kansas**: Overland. **Kentucky**: Lexington, Louisville (2). **Louisiana**: Baton Rouge, Harvey, Metairie (2). **Maryland**: Annapolis, Baltimore (2), Glen Burnie. **Mississippi**: Jackson. **Missouri**: Bridgeton, Overland Plaza, St. Charles, St. Louis (4), Springfield. **Nebraska**: Omaha (2). **North Carolina**: Charlotte (2), Durham, Greensboro. **Ohio**: Dayton (2). **Oklahoma**: Midwest City, Oklahoma City (2), Tulsa (2). **Pennsylvania**: Bethel Park, Edgewood, Rosa Township, West Mifflin. **South Carolina**: Charleston, Greeneville. **Tennessee**: Chattanooga, Knoxville, Madison, Nashville. **Texas**: Arlington (2), Austin (2), Corpus Christi, Dallas (4), Fort Worth, Garland, Houston (10), Irving, North Richland Hills, Plano, San Antonio (3). **Wisconsin**: Appleton, Brookfield, Green Bay, Greenfield.

Office Square, 7909 Fredricksburg Rd, San Antonio, TX 78229, telephone (800) 752-0726; FAX (800) 848-7205. *Stores:* **Illinois**: Bloomingdale, Deerfield, Platine. **Ohio**: Canton, Cuyahoga Falls.

The O.P. Club, 5125 N. 16th St, Suite A208, Phoenix, AZ 85016, telephone (602) 234-0334. *Stores:* **Arizona**: Phoenix (5). **California**: San Diego (2). **Utah**: Midvale, Salt Lake City.

OW Office Warehouse, Inc.., 308 Constitution Drive, Virginia Beach, VA 23462, telephone (804) 671-3379; FAX (804) 671-2232. *Stores:* **Arkansas**: Little Rock. **New Jersey**: Pennsaukin, Somerdale. **New York**: Albany, Buffalo (2), Poughkeepsie. **North Carolina**: Charlotte, Raleigh. **Pennsylvania**: Bristol, Harrisburg, Rising Sun, Wilkes-Barre, Willow Grove. **Rhode Island**: Providence. **South Carolina**: Columbia (2), Greenville. **Tennessee**: Memphis (2), Nashville. **Virginia**: Chesapeake, Hampton, Richmond (2), Virginia Beach.

The Paper Cutter, 4577 Buckley Road, Liverpool, NY 13088-2594, telephone (800) 388-8434; FAX (800) 388-8450. *Stores:* **New York:** Albany (4), Ithaca, New Hartford, Plattsburgh, Rochester, Syracuse (3).

Quill Corporation, 100 Schelter Rd, Lincolnshire, IL 60069-3621, telephone (708) 634-4800; FAX (708) 634-5708. West of the Rockies, telephone (714) 988-3200; FAX (708) 634-5708. *Warehouses:* **California:** Ontario. **Illinois:** Lincolnshire. **Canada:** Mississauga.

Staples, 150 California St, P. O. Box 160, Newton, MA 02195, Telephone (617) 969-3901; FAX (617) 558-5158. *Stores:* **California:** Anaheim/Fullerton (C.D. store), Cypress, Fountain Valley, La Mirada, North Hollywood, Norwalk, Orange, Santa Ana. **Note: as mentioned above, Staples has purchased the HQ Office Supplies operation in California and by the time this goes to print, will probably be operating the following additional store points there** - Alhambra, Bellflower, City of Industry, Culver City, Fullerton, Montebello, West Los Angeles, Woodland Hills, San Bernardino. **Connecticut:** Hamden, Newington, Norwalk, Stratford, West Hartford, West Haven, Wilton. **Kentucky:** Florence. **Maryland:** New Carrolton, Rockville (2), Silver Springs. **Massachusetts:** Boston (2), Brighton, Natick, Saugus, Seekonk, Waltham, Weymouth, West Springfield, Woburn. **New Hampshire:** Nashua, Salem. **New Jersey:** Cherry Hill, Livingston, Marlton, North Brunswick, North Plainfield, Paramus, Parsippany, Secaucus, Springfield, Totowa. **New York:** Carle Place, East Islip, Farmingdale, Freeport, Henrietta, (C.D. store), Hicksville, Irondequoit, Manhattan, Port Chester, Smithtown, Yonkers. **Ohio:** Cincinnati, Columbus (3), Springdale (C.D. store). **Pennsylvania:** Allentown (C.D. store), Bensalem, Bryn Mawr, King of Prussia, Montgomeryville, Oxford Valley, Philadelphia, Springfield, Valley Forge, Willow Grove. **Rhode Island:** Providence, Warwick. **Virginia:** Alexandria, Bailey's Crossroads, Manassas, Springfield, Tysons Corner.

Viking Office Products, 13809 S. Figueroa St, P. O. Box 6114, Los Angeles, CA 96661-0144, telephone (800) 421-1222; (800) 762-7329 FAX. *Stores:* **California**: Los Angeles. **Connecticut**: Windsor. **Florida**: Jacksonville. **New York**: New York City. **Ohio**: Cincinnati. **Texas**: Dallas.

WORKplace, 2004 34th Street North, St. Petersburg, FL 33713, telephone (813) 327-2292; (813) 321-1966 FAX. *Stores:* **Florida**: Brandon, Clearwater, Pinellas Park, Port Richey, Tampa (2).

SHOPPING AND ORDERING

If you live in one of the cities shown for one or more of the above vendors, you will find it (or them) listed in your local telephone directory. If none of them has a listing near you, call the home office numbers listed for a catalog or to place an order.

Chapter 15

LEGAL ASSISTANCE

Whether you are an average working person, a retired senior citizen, a small businessman, a professional or a housewife, chances are you will require some kind of legal service—major or minor—within the near future. This need may be as simple as requiring the service of a notary public, as complex as a liability lawsuit, or anything in between.

Unfortunately, the legal industry in the United States—and it is an industry—working with willing cohorts in the state legislatures and Congress has created a complex, costly, overly-regulated and litigious society.

Some states (California is an example) are at long last taking some small steps to reverse—or at least slow down—this shameful situation by allowing people other than full-fledged attorneys to handle specified routine legal matters. But, until the happy day comes when legislative and legal common sense is far more prevalent that it is today, all each of us can do is try to keep our legal exposure and expenses to a minimum.

SOMETIMES A LAWYER IS NECESSARY

There well may be a time when you need a lawyer. You might be involved in a criminal or civil proceeding where you have no choice, or in a complex business situation where it would be silly to proceed without competent legal counsel. If there is a large amount of money or property at stake, or if there is a possibility that the matter could end up in court, you probably would be well-advised to engage a competent attorney.

There are many situations, however, which you can handle without hiring a high priced legal eagle—either on your own or by using some qualified person who is not a member of the bar. For the most part, these are routine business or personal matters that have just been made to *sound* difficult by—who else—lawyers who would like to stick you with a big bill for doing very little. This chapter will give you pointers on some of the things you can do without a lawyer, starting with the very simple.

In cases where you do need a lawyer, we will provide information on the relatively new concept of prepaid legal services. This development is particularly helpful to small business owners just starting up, and to individuals who need legal assistance on a regular or periodic basis.

ARBITRATION

If you are involved in a dispute and both parties are interested in having it settled fairly with a minimum of legal expense, you could consider taking the matter to an impartial organization for mediation or arbitration. Information on organizations providing this type of service can be obtained from your local Better Business Bureau, or by calling the American Arbitration Association at (212) 484-4000.

SMALL CLAIMS

If you are involved in a dispute in which there is not a large amount of money or property involved, you can handle the matter yourself by taking it to small claims court. The monetary value handled by these courts varies from state to state and runs from $100 to $5000. You can obtain information on the limits in your state and the procedure you need to follow and the forms and filings required by calling or writing the County Clerk's Office at your local County Courthouse.

DO IT YOURSELF

There are many regulatory and routine legal matters which professionals, small business owners, and private individuals can handle themselves with the proper information. In some cases, it is merely a matter of finding out which forms and procedures to use. This can usually be determined by talking to the office, bureau, or agency involved. After all, the people who work there *are* public servants whose job it is to serve the public. Don't hesitate to ask questions. Be persistent—keep after it until you have all the information you need to handle the matter to a conclusion.

Larger stationery stores, especially those catering to legal offices and businesses, carry many standard legal forms such as leases, powers of attorney, promissory notes, stock transfers, etc. Unless you have an unusual circumstance, there is no point in paying a lawyer to draw up a special contract when a standard form will do the job just as well.

OTHER HELP

For other situations, there are plenty of self-help books and other publications available. Because laws vary from state to state, you should check with your local public library for those which apply in your state on the subject matter of interest. If you don't find what you need there, or if you would like to add to your own bookshelf, contact **Nolo Press,** 950 Parker Street, Berkeley, CA 94710 and request a catalog of their offerings. Nolo has some excellent publications to help reduce or eliminate legal costs.

PREPAID LEGAL SERVICES

Legal service plans as a method of providing needed legal services at reduced rates to consumers began receiving attention in the 1950's, but did not begin to proliferate until the 1970's. According to the American Prepaid Legal Services Institute, 13 million Americans were covered by a prepaid legal service plan by the end of 1987. Membership is no doubt several million higher today. Although many members are covered through plans offered by their employer or other organization, plans are available for private individuals and businesses.

Although there is some variation between plans, most of them operate somewhat like group insurance. For a given monthly or annual membership fee, the member receives specified routine legal services at no additional charge. For legal needs beyond the scope of those covered by the plan, the member receives a substantial discount from normal rates.

One Example: The following example of an actual plan will show in general how these plans work:

American Legal Network, 2049 Century Park East, Suite 4060, Los Angeles, CA 90067-3237, (213) 557-1504 offers a plan which provides the following services to clients in Los Angeles, San Francisco, San Diego and Orange County for no additional charge beyond the annual fee: Unlimited telephone consultation with an attorney (via an 800 number), unlimited document review, simple will, minor's trust, simple divorce, quitclaims, grant deeds, trust deeds, real estate documents, articles of incorporation, partnership agreements, promissory notes, general & special powers of attorney, and demand letters.

In addition, this group provides to its members general legal services for items not listed above at $70.00 per hour, far below the going rates of $100 to $200 or more per hour charged by attorneys in that area. If a specialist attorney is needed for a particular problem, American Legal will obtain one for its members at 25% to 50% off their usual and customary rates.

For More Information: The foregoing is offered as an example only. To get the names and addresses of other prepaid legal service plans, contact **American Prepaid Legal Service Institute**, 750 North Lake Shore Drive, Chicago, IL 60611, tel. (312) 988-5751, and ask for their list of *Organizations Offering Personal Legal Service Plans to Consumers and Groups*.

Membership fees in the prepaid legal plans vary, but most charge less than $200 per year for basic coverage. In some plans (American Legal Network is an example), members paying by American Express receive a 30% discount.

If you have, or expect to have, more than a modicum of legal work, membership in one of these groups will save you money. The annual membership fee is about what you could expect to pay for one or two hours legal work at so-called "usual and customary" rates.

HIRING A LAWYER

If you find yourself in a legal situation which you don't feel confident handling yourself and you are not a member of a prepaid individual or company legal plan, you will want to engage an attorney who (1) is competent, (2) is honest, (3) is a specialist in the type problem you have, (4) will carry out your wishes, and (5) will help you keep legal costs as low as possible.

Point five—keeping costs as low as possible—will probably be the most difficult of these goals to achieve. The simple truth is that if you are paying by the hour—a typical arrangement—it is in the perceived economic interest of the lawyer to string out matters and run up as many hours as possible. This could be called conflict of interest, but it is one conflict that won't bother your attorney a great deal.

Selecting the right lawyer is the first key, then reaching an understanding on fees and other issues is next on the list. In a given community, fees for particular types of legal work will be fairly consistent. And, since delays or the wrong outcome to a legal problem could more than offset any potential hourly savings achieved by hiring the cheapest lawyer around, it is important to choose right in the beginning.

Ask The Man Who Has Hired One: A good starting point is to ask people who know. These can be people who have had the same problem or are in the same business as you. If its an insurance problem ask two or three insurance brokers for a recommendation, if it has to do with real estate ask a realtor friend or two, if it is a commercial matter ask your local Chamber of Commerce, and so on.

Get a list of two or three names, then talk to each of them either in person or by telephone. Determine whether you would feel comfortable working with this person. Talk about fees up front, and reach an understanding as to whether charges will be by the hour (which means any fraction thereof), a flat fee, or contingent fee. Don't be bashful in setting a reasonable limit and getting the lawyer to agree to it. There's no point in spending $1000 in legal costs to collect an $800 debt, for example. Request the attorney to put in writing to you the points covered in your conversation, including in particular the fee arrangement. Reputable ones will gladly do so. The other kind you don't need.

Chapter 16

A FEW OTHER THINGS

The preceding chapters have covered products and services which constitute the bulk of purchases of the average American consumer. Use of the information provided there should result in literally thousands of dollars of savings. This chapter will list a few additional thrift suggestions.

BOOKS

As Chapter 26 will point out, your local libraries offer the best value on books which you want to read but don't necessarily want to own. For savings on books you want to purchase—but just can't wait to get—check the bookstores in your area, including independents and chains, for any specials or sales they might have going. If you're willing to take a little extra time in order to save money, check out the following suggestions.

Low Mail Order Prices: For mail order convenience and low prices, contact the following and get on their catalog mailing lists. Discounts up to 50% and even higher are offered on many of their listings:

* **Barnes & Noble,** 126 Fifth Avenue, New York, NY 10011, telephone (800) 242-6657.

* **Publishers Central Bureau**, Dept. 476, One Champion Avenue, Avenel, NJ 07001-2301, telephone (800) 722-9800, ext. 476.

Book Clubs: Another alternative is a book club membership. Almost everyone is familiar with the Book-of-the-Month Club, but there are literally dozens of other book clubs, most of them specializing in a field of particular interest. For a complete list of these, go to the reference section of your local library and ask for **Literary Market Place, The Directory of the American Book Publishing Industry,** published by R. R. Bowker. This publication has a listing of book clubs, broken down into adult and juvenile categories.

CEMETERY LOTS

See comments under Funerals below.

CRUISES AND TOURS

Many things affect prices in the travel industry, not the least of which is supply and demand. Supply and demand are influenced by a lot of factors, including the condition of the economy and the state of world politics. A case in point was the conflux of the Gulf War and the U. S. recession when bargains galore on cruise ships became endemic.

When planning a trip, be flexible in your timing if you can. Unsold space on cruise ships or tour buses gets cheaper as departure time draws nearer. Cruises are sold through travel agents, and some agents can offer a better deal than others. Travel agents which do a large volume of business with a particular cruise company can usually offer the best price.

As with any other purchase, shop around and compare. Some of the travel advisory services listed in Chapter 11 have telephone numbers you can call for last minute special deals.

EDUCATION

There appears to be no end to the ever-spiraling costs of college. That in itself is sufficient reason to spend a little time and effort in shopping around. Another good reason is that it is entirely possible to obtain a *better* education at some of the smaller, less-expensive schools than at the better known bastions of higher learning.

One way to shave costs, of course, is to spend the first couple of years at a two-year community, or junior, college. This is particularly true for students who are not at all sure that they want to spend four years in college, anyway, and just "sort of want to give college a try."

Another way is to enroll in a cooperative education program which combines classroom work with a part-time job. In addition to helping pay tuition costs, this approach has the advantage of giving the student a dose of real-life experience which will serve him/her well after graduation. For information on co-op education, contact the **National Commission for Cooperative Education,** 360 Huntington Avenue, Boston, MA 02115 and request a free copy of *Co-op Education Undergraduate Program Directory*.

College Guides: It is helpful to narrow down the list of potential colleges or universities before undertaking an in-depth comparison including campus visits. To this end, the following publications are recommended:

* *The National Review College Guide*. Sub-titled *America's 50 Top Liberal Arts Schools*. Available from National Review College Guide, 150 East 35th Street, New York, NY 10016, telephone (212) 679-7330. Primarily concerned with "educational philosophy, purpose and the quality of campus life," but tuition cost information is included so price comparisons are possible. Price $14.95 (plus $2.00 s&h).

* *The Public Ivys*, by Richard Moll. Published by Viking Penguin, 40 West 23rd Street, New York, NY 10010. Price $7.95. Covers public colleges and universities which the author feels offer an education comparable to Ivy League schools, with tuition costs one-third to one-half the latter. Check your local public library. If not available there, try a local bookstore or contact the publisher.

ENTERTAINMENT

Most movie houses and many other types of entertainment offer discounts to students and senior citizens. Many movie theaters have lower prices for matinee performances for all patrons—take advantage of these when you can.

For other theater tickets at a discount, you can buy day-of-performance tickets at a 50% discount for many shows if you live in or near (or plan to visit) one of the following cities. The name and telephone number (if they have a listing) of the discount ticket agency is shown for each location:

* **Boston**: Bostix (617) 723-5181
* **Chicago**: Hottix (312) 977-1755
* **Denver**: Ticket Bus (16th Street Mall)
* **New York City**: Theater Development (212) 354-5800
* **Pittsburgh**: Tix (412) 642-2787
* **Philadelphia**: Cultural Connection (215) 564-4414
* **San Diego**: Artstix (619) 238-3810
* **San Francisco**: STBS (415) 433-7827
* **Washington, DC:** Ticket Place (202) 842-5387

FUNERALS

Cemetery lots and funerals are items which almost everyone will purchase—or have purchased for him—sooner or later. But, all too often these are not acquired until they are needed, at which point the person responsible for making the arrangements is not in the proper frame of mind to pay proper attention to costs. Nor does he or she have time to shop around and compare products, services, and prices.

As the last major expenditure each of us will make (or have made on our behalf) on this earth, we should do necessary planning, make as many decisions as possible, and leave full information and instructions regarding these matters. If it is left to someone else to do, they will probably end up spending much more money than you would have wished—money they could better use for their future support.

For information which will assist you in this, write for the following brochures:

* *Consumer Guide to the FTC Funeral Rule*, Consumer Information Center, Pueblo, CO 81009 (price $0.50).

* The American Association of Retired Persons (AARP), 1909 K Street NW, Washington, DC has the following free bulletins available: *Cemetery Goods and Services; Funeral Goods and Services;* and *Pre-Paying Your Funeral Expenses.*

You may also contact the Conference of Funeral Service Examining Boards, P. O. Box 497, Washington, IN 47501, (812) 254-7887, for the name and address of the licensing board which regulates the funeral industry in your state. This board will be able to provide you with information relative to funeral laws which apply where you live.

The point is to be armed with plenty of facts before starting to collect price and other information from local providers of these services.

HOME REPAIRS

For minor repairs around the house, take a crack at doing them yourself before calling an expensive serviceman. If you are handy at all with tools you can do many of these with the assistance of self-help instruction manuals on sale at most home-improvement centers and hardware stores.

If its a job you feel you should have someone else do, use a reputable, qualified repair service. Avoid unknown pitchmen who show up at your front door or call on the telephone. Ask your friends or neighbors for a recommendation, or use a contractor referral organization which you can find in the yellow pages under home repairs. Or, call the contractor licensing bureau in your community and ask for a referral.

HOSPITALS

The type of room you get in a hospital—private, semi-private, or ward—will have a major impact on your total bill. Most group insurance policies specify the maximum amount payable for rooms. Stay within this limit if at all possible, unless you are willing to make up the difference.

Check all hospital bills item by item before paying them, especially charges for medication. Ask the attending physician for confirmation if you have any doubts. Unfortunately, padded hospital bills are not unknown and medical costs are high enough without paying for something you didn't get.

MEDICINES

Probably no single commodity group purchased by the public has a wider range of prices for identical products than that of prescription drugs. Surveys by organizations such as Consumer's Union, the American Medical Association and others have turned up price differences as much as 900% in one city! A price disparity of this magnitude may not be common, but differences of 25% to 300% are quite frequent.

There are a few simple steps you can take to keep from getting ripped off on prescriptions. First, if you have group health insurance, find out if the insurance company or your employer has a special arrangement with a prescription service. Many of them do.

Second, if your doctor approves, ask for the generic equivalent of brand name drugs when available. Brand name drugs can cost up to seven times the generic equivalent, according to the Department of Health and Human Services.

Third, shop and compare. You can do this by telephone. Look in the yellow pages for at least three pharmacies and call and ask what their price would be for your prescription. If one or more of the chain discount drug operators has stores in your area, include them in your list. These are: Cost Cutters, dot, Drug Emporium, Drugs for Less, Drug Palace, Drug World,

F&M, Freddy's, Marc's, Phar-More, Pic N'Save Drug Stores, A. L. Price, Rockbottom, Rx Palace, and Sid's.

Some of the warehouse clubs listed in Chapter 7 also have a pharmacy department. And, for seniors, refer to the benefits offered by some of the senior citizen organizations listed in Chapter 25.

NOTARY PUBLIC

Laws in most states require that many routine documents have signatures notarized by a Notary Public. Notary fees per signature can run from $2.00 to $10.00 or more. There are sources which will provide this service free of charge, or at reduced rates. When you need a Notary, check with one of the organizations with which you do business or to which you belong, such as: bank or savings & loan, credit union, your employer, auto club, or social or service clubs. Many of these are glad to perform this service for their customers or members at no charge.

PROBATE COSTS

Legal fees to probate an estate can be ridiculously high. To significantly reduce (or eliminate) these fees, refer to the comments under Estate and Inheritance Taxes in Chapter 7.

STOCKBROKERS

If you trade in the stock market and are the sort who makes his own investment decisions (you probably shouldn't be in the market if you don't), check out the difference in commission costs between your regular broker and a discount broker. Discount brokers normally charge a fraction of regular broker's fees. You can get the names and telephone numbers from one of the financial journals, the business section of your newspaper, the yellow pages, or the reference section of your local library.

VACATIONS

Other than getting there, the cost of your vacation abode will no doubt eat up the largest chunk of your holiday budget—unless you camp out or stay with friends or relatives. An alternative to expensive hotels or resorts is the use of privately owned villas, condos or homes which are available through organizations which specialize in arranging rentals or exchanges of these types of properties. Following are two such organizations:

Condolink, 7701 Pacific Street, Omaha, NE 68114-5489, telephone (800) 733-4445 or (402) 392-0468. Condolink acts as agent for fully furnished condos in resort locations throughout the United States, Mexico, the Caribbean and Europe. They claim to be the nation's largest condominium rental source, with an inventory of over 75,000 units. Depending on location, a wide variety of price ranges are available, from $75.00 per day budget units to $750.00 per day luxury spreads. Condolink can also provide travel service, if desired.

Hideaways International, 15 Goldsmith Street, P. O. Box 1270, Littleton, MA 01460, telephone (800) 843-4433 or (508) 486-8955 in Massachusetts. Hideaways is a membership operation which offers what could best be described as up-market alternative vacations, ranging from villas and condominiums to apartments in Paris or yachts and special cruises. A membership, which costs $79.00 per year, provides quarterly newsletters plus bi-annual directories. The directories are well done, with photos, full descriptions, and prices. A four-month trial membership, which includes one directory, is available for $27.50. A travel service is offered, but is not mandatory.

Other Sources: Some of the travel advisory publications listed in Chapter 11 provide information on other sources of low-priced holiday housing from time to time.

Chapter 17

AUCTIONS

Auctions are popular with sellers because they provide an outlet for goods for which there are often no other satisfactory marketing channels, they allow for the movement of a large number of items in a short time frame, and they offer an immediate and permanent solution to the seller of the goods (there are no warranties and no returns).

Buyers like auctions because they perceive that bargains may be had there, and because sometimes an auction is the best—or only—source for a particular item. In addition, an auction is something of a social occasion. It provides entertainment to the participants—sometimes, when bidding becomes fierce—in the form of high drama.

AUCTION SPONSORS

Auctions are used by federal, state and local governments; bankruptcy courts; estate liquidators; individuals; corporations; public utilities and others to dispose of almost every kind of property imaginable. You can get information about auctions in your area by watching for notices in local newspapers, or by calling auction companies (listed under Auctioneers) in your telephone yellow pages and asking to be placed on their mailing list.

You may also contact your state consumer information office and determine whether it publishes a directory of licensed auction companies or auctioneers. Several states have an "Auctioneers Commission" or similar official body which licenses auctioneers and can provide you with a list of them. Information on how to get on the mailing lists for various U. S. Government auctions is given in Chapter 22.

Notices of auctions will usually give the location, date and time when the merchandise may be inspected prior to the auction date. If motor vehicles are involved, the notice will normally state a date and time for "motor starting." Note that other than visual inspection, starting and listening to the engine is the only demonstration which you will be allowed.

Follow the Rules to Find a Bargain: There is a widespread belief that tremendous bargains are to be had at auctions, especially those selling off goods or lands as a result of bankruptcy or death, or those disposing of surplus or seized Government property. This latter category, especially, is being somewhat misleadingly hyped by promoters using TV spot advertisements and other media ads.

Bargain buys at auctions *are* possible—but only by disciplined people who follow certain well-defined rules. Observing these rules should at least keep you from getting burned at auctions, and may even help you end up with that rare "stupendous bargain." These rules are:

[1] Inspect the item in which you are interested *before* the date of the auction. Check it over carefully. If it is a motor vehicle take your mechanic with you on "motor starting" day, unless you're an expert yourself.

[2] Collect all the market intelligence possible,including the going market rate for a like item in similar condition elsewhere.

[3] Become acquainted with the rules of the auction. They will usually be explained by the auctioneer before the auction begins, and/or may be printed in the catalog or program. Remember, under the rules and regulations governing auctions in most states, a bid is considered a binding offer—if you raise your hand or otherwise signal the auctioneer, you may have bought yourself a 1933 Fire Engine whether you intended to or not.

[4] Establish the maximum amount you are willing to pay *before* the auction begins—and stick to it! Don't get carried away in the heat of battle and end up paying more than an item is worth. Many people do. That's one reason auctions are popular with sellers.

[5] Finally, remember that if you end up as the successful bidder it will be because you paid more for the item than anyone else was willing to. Whether that is more than you should have paid will depend on how well you followed rules 1 through 4.

GOVERNMENT AUCTIONS

Sales of U. S. Government surplus and other property at auction are covered in more detail in the Chapter 22 U. S. Government Property.

Chapter 18

CATALOG SHOPPING

Shopping by catalog was probably the first direct marketing system. Direct marketing is the selling of goods by vendors who by-pass the usual wholesale/retail marketing chain. Under this system merchandise may be ordered by mail, telephone, fax, or computer. Most direct marketers provide their prospects with catalogs or brochures describing their wares. Some provide information on their products via personal computer networks or television shopping channels. These are covered in Chapter 19 *Electronic Shopping.*

The direct order business has grown tremendously in the past few years. It is estimated that there are presently more than 13,000 direct order firms in the United States. Consumers are flocking to this way of doing business not only for cost savings and convenience, but because they are fed up with high prices and poor service encountered in many retail establishments. Sellers are switching to direct marketing because of high fixed operating costs, and because it is becoming increasingly difficult and expensive to hire qualified sales people.

SHOPPING FROM HOME

Buying from a catalog, TV screen, or computer often affords considerable savings to the buyer. By eliminating one or more middlemen, the vendor can pass its commission savings on to you. It is also convenient—especially if you are one of those people who hate to shop—and it saves wear and tear on yourself and on your automobile.

Caution: There are some things you should bear in mind when buying in this manner. If you haven't dealt with the firm you are ordering from, you may be taking a chance on the reliability and integrity of the seller. (The Better Business Bureau of

Metropolitan New York reports that the mail order business leads the list of consumer complaints received by them). And, unless you are ordering by brand name and model number, there is always the chance that the merchandise received will not measure up to expectations.

Suggestions: Deal only with well-known, reputable firms, or with those recommended by people you trust; and, whenever possible, order by brand name, model number, type, color or other specific description.

If you are not familiar with a firm you would like to order from—and have no friends or associates who can recommend it—check with the Better Business Bureau in the city where it is located to see whether there have been any complaints recorded against it. BBB's will level with you—it is in the interest of the reputable firms in their area to do so.

When shopping from catalogs—whether printed or electronic— we recommend that you read and heed the following guidelines:

[1] As emphasized throughout this report, *always compare prices* (including shipping and handling charges), not only with your local retail or discount stores, but with other catalogs and discount shopping services as well.

[2] Make sure the seller has a "no weasel" money-back guarantee in case you are not satisfied with the merchandise.

[3] Always pay by credit card, if possible. This allows some protection in the event of a disagreement or improper shipment. If the vendor doesn't accept credit cards, pay by check or money order. *Never pay with cash.*

[4] Keep complete records of the transaction, including the date ordered, the vendor's order number, the method of payment, price quoted (including shipping and handling), and promised delivery time. If ordered by telephone, write down the name of the person you talked to. This information will be required in case a problem develops.

[5] Give your street address as the SHIP TO address, not a post office box. Most vendors ship via UPS or Federal Express which do not deliver to a postal box.

If you follow the guidelines given above, shopping by catalog can be easy and profitable. If a problem does occur which you are unable to resolve with the vendor, refer to Chapter 28 *Consumer Protection Agencies.*

CATALOG SOURCES

The sources listed below will assist you in finding a direct mail seller for practically any item imaginable. Many of them offer considerable savings compared to local retail shops. The first four guides listed were compiled and published with the consumer in mind. Check your local public library to see if they have some—or all of these. Many of them do. If it doesn't—or even if it does—you may want to buy one or more of these guides to keep on hand for ready reference.

The 3rd Underground Shopper, by Sue Goldstein, published by Andrews, McMeel & Parker, Kansas City - New York. 532 pages, $8.95. This jam-packed little book is the third edition of a most successful endeavor. The first edition was published in 1983 under the title *The Underground Shopper: A Guide to Discount Mail-Order Shopping*, and sold more than 100,000 copies.

Contents include: apparel; appliances & TVs; art & collectibles; art supplies; bed & bath; boating supplies; cameras, opticals & photographic equipment; carpets & rugs; cars & auto supplies; catalog showrooms; china; crystal & silver; computers & electronics; cosmetics & beauty aids; fabrics; fitness & health; food; freebies; furniture & accessories; handbags & luggage; hard-to-find & unique items; hardware & tools; hobbies & crafts; housewares; investments; jewelry; kits & kaboodle (do-It-Yourself); medical products & supplies; musical instruments; novelties; office supplies; pet & ranch animals; plants, flowers, gardens, & farming; records & tapes; shoes; sporting goods; stereo & video; surplus & volume sales; telephone services; tobacco; toys; travel; and windows & walls.   Other sections useful to consumers who shop by mail are included.

S&B Shop by Mail, The S&B Report, 112 East 36th St., 4th Floor, New York, NY 10016. One-year subscription (4 issues), $18.00. This booklet lists approximately 200 manufacturers and distributors. Savings of 40% to 70% are advertised.

Merchandise list includes: carpeting & rugs; home appliances; furniture; china; silver; crystal; fabrics; lighting fixtures; sheets & towels; cameras; perfumes & toiletries; clothing; watches; window treatment; home accessories; giftwear; cooking & kitchenware; wallcoverings; leather accessories; and electronic equipment.

For those who live in the New York city area (or plan to visit there), this organization also produces *The S&B Report*, a monthly publication which lists between 75 and 200 New York designer showroom sales each month. Savings of 50% to 70% on such items as women's & men's clothing, jewelry & accessories, children's clothing, furs, furniture & household, and appliances & electronics are listed.

Shop By Mail Worldwide, by Anne Flato & Marilyn Schiff, Vintage Books, A Division of Random House, New York, NY. (A Book-Of-The-Month-Club offering).   If you are into Waterford crystal, Royal Doulton China, Hummel figurines or any of hundreds of other quality products produced abroad, this 290 page guide is for you.

It lists foreign sources for clothing; food; furniture; jewelry; lighting fixtures; linens; perfumes; silver, and other items. In addition, it includes information on ordering from foreign sources and covers some of the pitfalls to watch for. Unfortunately, we are told by the publisher that this book is presently out of stock and is probably going out of print. If you are fortunate, your local library will have a copy.

The Wholesale By Mail Catalog, by The Print Project. For information: St. Martins Press, 175 Fifth Avenue, New York, NY 10010, 464 pages, $10.95. This publication has more than 500 entries and carries the bold statement that "You can buy almost anything at 30% to 90% off retail prices - by mail!" In addition to the listing of firms and products it, too, contains valuable information for using mail order.

Listings include: animal; appliances, audio, TV & video; art, antiques, & collectibles; art material; auto & marine; books, magazines, records & tapes; cameras, photographic & darkroom equipment, optics, film, & services; cigars, pipes, tobacco, & other smoking needs; clothing; maternity, infant's, & children's clothing; crafts & hobbies; farm & garden; food & drink; general merchandise, gifts, & buying clubs; health & beauty; home decor, furnishings, kitchen, linen, maintenance, table settings); jewelry, gems, & watches; leather goods; medical & scientific; music; office & computing; sports & recreation; surplus; tools, hardware, electronics, energy, safety, security, & industrial; and toys & games.

Almost all the companies listed in the foregoing directories publish catalogs or other written advertising materials which are available upon request, many without charge. However, in the event you would like to have a comprehensive list of catalogs readily available, you might be interested in the "catalogs of catalogs" which follow:

Catalogs Of Catalogs: Here is a listing of catalogs which may be ordered—for a price.

Nationwide Shopper Catalogs, Published by Nationwide Shopping Systems, Inc., P. O. Box 4507, Burbank, CA 91502, Price $6.00. Lists over 300 catalogs available from vendors, covering many areas of interest. Some catalogs listed are free, others cost from $1.00 upwards. Some of the sellers which charge for their catalog rebate the cost on your first order.

International Catalogue Collection, also published by Nationwide Shopping Systems, Inc. (see above), price $6.00. A collection of exporters, manufacturers and shops in foreign countries. Items such as art, antiques, clothing, linens, lace, specialty foods, etc. are included.

Shop The World By Mail, Box 5549, Cary., NC 27511-5549, Price: $4.00. If your library doesn't have a copy of *Shop by Mail Worldwide* (listed previously), or if that particular catalog doesn't have the supplier or item you are looking for, perhaps you should try this publication. It, too, is a "catalog of catalogs" covering more than 100 factories and shops in over 25 countries. It includes foreign suppliers of china, crystal, clothing, handicrafts, jewelry, linens, perfumes and other items.

ADDITIONAL SOURCES

If you didn't find the items you wanted in one of the foregoing publications, one of the volumes which follow may answer your need. Each of them contains the names and addresses of literally thousands of firms in the mail order business. They are intended primarily for the business market, and are priced accordingly. For that reason the average consumer will probably not be buying them for his bookshelf. But, if you would like to use them, you can probably find one (or more) in the reference section of your local public or college library.

The Directory of Mail Order Catalogs, Richard Gottlieb, Publisher, Grey House Publishing, Lakeville, CT 06039, 363 pages, $135.00. This directory lists more than 7,000 active mail order companies, including those which describe their products in brochures and fliers as well as those which issue catalogs. It comes equipped with two indexes—one by product, the other by company. It has one other feature which could be useful if you have difficulty in solving a problem with a mail order firm—it contains not only company names and addresses, but the names of owners, executives, buyers, and marketing managers.

Inside The Leading Mail Order Houses, by Maxwell Sroge with Bradley Highum, NTC Business Books, A Division of National Textbook Company, Lincolnwood, IL 630 pages, $89.95. This book is for business people who are in, or doing business with, mail order firms. However, it provides some insights and statistics regarding the mail order business which consumers will find of interest. Only 300 companies (of more than 13,000) mail order organizations are included in this report, but these conduct an estimated 40% of total U. S. mail order business.

Mail Order Business Directory, Klein Publications, P. O. Box 8503, Coral Springs, FL 33065, 450 pages, $75.00. More than 10,000 mail order and catalog houses are listed in this business-oriented directory, including many Canadian and overseas mail order companies. Companies are listed geographically. An indication of the types of products handled follows each listing.

Chapter 19

ELECTRONIC SHOPPING

To the computer buff, shopping electronically might mean dialing one of several computer networks via modem and scrutinizing lists of products on the screen of his monitor before eventually placing an order—again via his personal computer— with the vendor of his choice.

To the housewife without a personal computer, electronic shopping could mean buying from a wide array of goods on one of the TV channels dedicated to merchandising.

Another mode of electronic shopping is, of course, the telephone. The consumer may receive a telemarketing pitch over the phone and buy the item being touted. Or, he may just pick up the telephone and call the vendor of his choice (hopefully using an 800 number) and place an order for the product wanted.

This chapter covers all three of these categories. The names and addresses (and/or telephone numbers) of some of the major players are given, and an indication of the kinds of goods available from each. Again, because the range of products and brands is so extensive, it is impossible to include a complete detailed listing for each category. If you need more information than that shown here, you should contact the appropriate organization.

SHOPPING BY COMPUTER

In step with the growing use of home based personal computers for business and pleasure, shopping by computer/modem via one of the network PC services is growing in popularity. If you have a PC equipped with a modem but haven't gotten into shopping this way yet, there are a couple of things you should be aware of: (1) not every vendor listed by the various shopping networks sells below list price, so you won't necessarily save money shopping this way, (2) if you have to pay a network accessing fee or surcharge, or a toll telephone charge, these could substantially eat into any savings.

To save on toll and connection charges, properly organize yourself before turning on your computer—have all the specifications written down, know which computer service (if you subscribe to more than one) you plan to use, and which vendor provided by that service is likely to have the merchandise you want.

It is possible to just browse some of these online markets if you don't know what you want or who the vendors are. Depending on which service you use, its surcharge policy, and whether you have to access by toll line, this may or may not be an economical thing to do. But, if you are one of those people who like to window shop, you may elect to do it anyway.

Computer Shopping Services

Listed below are some of the better known services which provide online shopping. **(Note:** Each network provides its subscribers a wide range of services in addition to shopping which are not covered in this report. Contact the individual network for more information).

CompuServe Information Services, 5000 Arlington Centre Boulevard, P. O. Box 20212, Columbus, OH. Tel. (800) 848-8199 or (617) 457-0802 within Ohio.

Literally thousands of products may be ordered via this service. CompuServe offers its clients access to *Shopper's Advantage* (known on other services as *Comp-u-Store*, which is described in more detail later in this chapter). In addition, CompuServe provides access to two other on-line shopping services—*The Electronic Mall,* consisting of more than 100 merchants handling almost every conceivable product, and *J. C. Penney*, the old line department store turned aggressive electronic marketeer.

Prodigy, A partnership of IBM and Sears, 45 Hamilton Avenue, White Plains, NY 10601. Tel. 1-800-822-6922 (or contact your local Sears store). Dozens of merchants are carried by this service, including such catalog services as Sears, J. C. Penney, and Spiegel. In addition to browsing and/or ordering, Prodigy helps it customers locate bargains by providing a daily Shopping Highlights list, and a Value Day on Friday of each week. Special sales are also featured by some merchants from time to time.

Other Connections: If you do not subscribe to one of the on-line networks listed above, you may still shop via your PC using one of the following:

Comp-u-Store OnLine, P.O. Box 1016, Trumbull, CT 06611-1016, Tel. (800) 843-7777, is a discount buying service made available by CUC International of Stamford, Connecticut via the following PC user networks: **America Online, Bell Atlantic, Bell South TUG, Delphi, Dow Jones/News Retrieval, GEnie, Minitel, PC Link, Q-Link, Tymnet, US West Community Link, US Videotel.**

There is an annual club membership fee of $39.00 for direct membership in Compu-u-Store. In addition, shoppers are assessed the network's standard time charge while shopping via computer by most of the network services while using this (or other) online shopping services. Fees vary—check with the service to which you subscribe for complete details.

Comp-u-Store offers its members more than 250,000 products at prices up to 10% to 50% less than manufacturers' suggested retail for such items as bed & bath; cars & auto accessories; computers & accessories; formal living & dining, home & office equipment; home furnishings; housewares; leisure; luxury; major appliances; photographic & optical equipment; sound products; tools & seasonal; and TV & video. It offers top quality products from well-known manufacturers, and backs its lowest price claim with a guarantee to rebate the difference if you see the identical product advertised for less within 30 days of your purchase.

For the Sporting Crowd: For products and services which are strictly sports related, including sports equipment, team sportswear, games, videos, books, PC accessories, college team T-shirts, and Pro jerseys, you might consider the following (available nationwide via **Tymnet** or **Telenet**): **USA Today Sports Center,** Four Seasons Executive Center, 9 Terrace Way, Greensboro, NC 27403, (800) 826-9688.

SHOPPING BY TELEPHONE

In the electronic shopping field, there is a certain amount of crossover. Some of the firms on computer networks also operate a telephone shopping service, either under the same or a different name. Also, the usual method of ordering goods sold by television shopping channels is by telephone. This crossing over extends to normal catalog shopping as well. Many, if not most, direct marketers who publicize their wares by catalog or brochure now accept telephone orders, many by toll-free 800 numbers. More about these 800 numbers later in this chapter. Following is a listing of some of the major telephone discount shopping services, together with descriptions of the goods which they handle.

LVT Price Quote Hotline, Inc. P. O. Box 444, Commack, NY 11725-0444, Tel. (516) 234-8884. As LVT says in its brochure, it combines the convenience of shopping at home with low prices. In addition, LVT does not charge a membership fee. If you know the brand, model number, etc. of the item you want to buy, just call or write LVT for a price quotation (their prices include surface shipping costs).

Unfortunately, LVT does not (as of this writing) have a toll-free 800 telephone number. Payment must be made in advance of shipment by cashier's check, certified check, Postal money order, or bank wire transfer. If you pay by personal check, expect a delay while the check clears. Credit cards are not accepted. This inconvenience may be more than offset by the savings you get.

Merchandise handled by this supplier includes air cleaners; air conditioners; audio components; calculators; cameras; coffee makers; computers; copying machines; appliances (major and small); fax machines, radar detectors, scanners, CB's; radios; telephone equipment;, typewriters; VCR's, and others.

Quota-Phone, 47 Halstead Avenue, Harrison, NY 10528, Tel. (800) 221-0626 or (914) 835-5300. A membership fee in Quota-Phone (which also uses the name **The Buying Service**) runs from $19.00 to $36.00 per year. Purchases may be made by credit card, check or C.O.D. Price quotes are available 24 hours a day, 7 days a week, with no obligation to buy.

Quota-Phone offers savings up to 40% on all kinds of merchandise, including: air conditioner; appliances; calculators; CB's, radar detectors, scanners; china; computers; crystal; jewelry; luggage; musical instruments; photo equipment; sewing machines; stereos & CD's; silverware; telephone equipment; TV's; typewriters; VCR's, video cameras, etc. In addition, they have discounts available on travel, prescription drugs, autos (new & used), car rental, and moving.

Shoppers Advantage, P. O. Box 1016, Turnbull, CT 06611, Tel. (800) 835-7467. Shoppers Advantage is a discount buying service provided by CUC International, and is the telephone counter-part to Comp-u-Store, listed previously under computer online shopping. There is an annual membership fee of $39.00, and membership is available to almost anyone who has a Mastercard or Visa card. Hours for toll-free shopping—or just getting a price quote—are 8:00am to midnight (ET) Monday-Friday, and 9:00am to 8:00pm Saturday & Sunday.

In addition to being available directly from CUC, this service is marketed through other channels, including some of the major banks (an example is CitiShopper available from Citibank).

CUC is one of the larger buying organizations in the U.S., and as such has considerable clout with their suppliers. Shoppers Advantage and its sister service make available hundreds of brand names offering more than 250,000 items,

including: appliances (major & small); clothing; linens &
towels; tools and lawn equipment; luxury goods; computers &
accessories; home furnishings; formal living & dining products
(silverware, china, crystal, flatware); office equipment; leisure
products; and TV & video equipment.   Discounts are also
available on new cars, car rentals, and real estate transactions.

TELEVISION SHOPPING

The remaining major players in the relatively new and popular
television shopping business are Home Shopping Club and QVC
Shopping Channel (J. C. Penney turned it's TV cable space over
to QVC in mid-1991).   Each of these has a TV cable channel
devoted exclusively to selling merchandise via the tube. Check
the local TV listings for channel numbers in your area.   For
those people who have the time to sit and watch, there are
bargains available from these vendors, but as we constantly
remind readers, shop and compare—TV prices are not always the
lowest.

Program   segment   schedules   which   show   the   types   of
merchandise advertised during particular time slots are available
from each of these vendors. To obtain one of these, or for other
information on any of these TV operations, you may contact
them at the addresses or telephone numbers shown:

Home Shopping Club, P. O. Box 9090, Clearwater, FL 34618,
(813) 572-8585.

QVC Network, Inc., 1365 Enterprise Drive, West Chester, PA
19380, (215) 430-1000.

A word of caution about TV shopping—although the brand is
usually mentioned, the manufacturer's model number is not
given. If you see an item in which you are interested, call the
800 number given on the screen and ask for the manufacturer's
model number. You will probably be able to get it, and can then
compare prices with your local retail discount shops and with

one or more of the buying services listed in this chapter. If the TV vendor does have the lowest price, there should be no objection to giving you the information you request—its to their advantage. If they refuse to provide this information, there must be a reason.

USING 800 TELEPHONE NUMBERS

Always use an 800 number, if available, when requesting information or ordering merchandise by telephone. Many of the companies which advertise by direct mail or advertise on TV provide 800 numbers for customers to use in placing orders or making inquiries. There is a growing number of other businesses and organizations which have toll-free numbers that can be used for buying goods, obtaining information, registering complaints, or filing a claim. This subject is covered in more detail in Chapter 3 *Household Utilities*.

Chapter 20

FACTORY OUTLETS

Factory outlet stores are rapidly spreading across the USA. Until fairly recently such outlets were more or less confined to small mill towns in the northeastern part of the country. From there they spread south, beginning in the early eighties, and have now made it across the country to the west coast.

Factory outlet malls, as they are usually called, continue to spring up in many sections of the country at a rapid rate. According to *The Joy of Outlet Shopping* (see listing below), there were at least 357 bonafide outlet chains with more than 6000 stores operating in 1990, and growth continues apace.

There are some good reasons for this, the major one being substantial savings on designer merchandise or other well-known brand names. Everyone loves a bargain, and these can be found in abundance in outlet stores—discounts range from 20% to 70% off normal retail prices.

WHAT THEY CARRY

At one time, outlets were considered (and often were) the manufacturer's method of disposing of inferior merchandise such as seconds or goods damaged in transit. Although this type of merchandise is still handled by some outlets, it's no longer the whole ball game. Many outlet stores stock first line goods—sometimes before department stores or other retailers get them.

A glance through one of the directories listed below should convince you that outlets are not hole-in-the-wall operations of unknown manufacturers. Listed are such top names as Adolfo, Anne Klein, Bass Shoe, Black & Decker, Calvin Klein, Corning/Revere, Dan River, Polo/Ralph Lauren, Springmaid Wamsutta, and many others.

WHERE THEY ARE

Because outlets are purposefully located at some distance from major metropolitan areas and do little in the way of advertising (to prevent friction with their major retail distributors), they were often hard to find. This problem has been solved by the publication of the following up-to-date directories which lists locations of outlet centers and gives the names of the manufacturers represented:

The Joy of Outlet Shopping, The Outlet Consumer Reporter, P.O. Box 7867, St. Petersburg, FL 33734 (Price: $4.95). This well-designed guide is indeed a joy! The book covers U. S. outlet centers from coast to coast and includes a map showing their locations. Listings are by state and city, followed by the exact location and, in many cases, days and hours of operation. This information is followed by a list of stores in each center.

Included is a ten page table listing 357 chains which the publisher has investigated and certified as true outlets. The types of merchandise and the range of discounts which can be expected are shown for each. Other information of interest, including a brief history of factory outlets and shopping tips, is included.

Outletbound, The Outlet Marketing Group, P. O. Box 1255, Orange, CT 06477, Tel. (800) 336-8853 or (800) 346-8853 (inside CT). (Price $5.95). Another attractive and up-to-date directory of factory outlets, *Outletbound* contains details on 277 outlet centers comprising more than 4500 factory direct stores, plus a section showing locations of planned new outlets by state and city. The book has charts showing types of products carried by each store, as well as a listing of the 70 top designer outlets.

The publisher of *Outletbound* has a telephone hot-line service which provides information on specific outlets, answers other questions on this subject, and will even help you plan your vacation trip so you can visit outlet centers along the way. Call the toll-free 800 numbers shown above to take advantage of this service.

OUTSIDE THE U.S.

The infatuation with factory outlet shopping is not confined to the United States, as the following will illustrate:

Canada: Residents in Ontario, and Americans living near the U.S./Ontario border will be interested in the *Buyers Guide to Factory Outlets and Off Price Outlets*, available from Oliver Enterprises, Box 2173, Cambridge, Ontario N3C 2V8, Canada (Price Can.$4.95 plus P&H $1.48).

This is an attractive and easy to use guide to more than 250 manufacturers outlets in the province of Ontario. An explanation as to what constitutes a factory outlet in Canada is included. Listings are by area, then outlet name and address.   The directory gives a rundown of the types of products carried by each store.

Great Britain: Inasmuch as clothing mills, which spawned the original outlet shops, first came into being in Great Britain during the industrial revolution, it should not be surprising that factory outlets (there called factory shops) are popular in that country as well.   Those of you planning a trip to Britain might be well advised to prepare yourself in advance by obtaining one or more of the factory shops guides available from **Gillian Cutress,** 34 Park Hill, London SW4 9PB, England, Telephone (01) 622-3722.

The following individual guides are available from this publisher: *Staffordshire & The Potteries; Derbyshire & Nottinghamshire; Western Midlands; Leicestershire & Northamptonshire; Yorkshire & Humberside; Northern England* (Cumbria, Tyne & Wear, Northumberland, Co. Durham, Cleveland); *Wales;* and *The North-West* (Lancashire, Cheshire, Greater Manchester, Merseyside). A pamphlet giving the price of each guide and containing information on what is available in each area may be obtained by contacting the publisher at the address shown above.

Chapter 21

WAREHOUSE MEMBERSHIP CLUBS

Membership warehouses, or wholesale clubs, are cash and carry operations which normally mark up merchandise about 10 percent above cost, compared to 25 percent or more for discount chains and 50 percent and up for other retailers. As a result of their lower prices, they are another extremely fast growing merchandising segment.

Goods sold by these operators usually are shipped directly from the manufacturer to the warehouse, reducing freight costs and cutting out distributors or other middlemen. There are no salesmen—customers serve themselves, goods are paid for in cash or check, and there are no fancy fixtures. All of these factors generate savings which are passed on to the customer. However, to obtain these savings the buyer may have to purchase some items in larger quantities than he would at other retailers.

Annual sales of discount clubs are estimated at $20 billion and growing. At the time this report goes to press, there will probably be more than 400 discount warehouses in operation in the U.S. with more being added constantly.

WHO CAN JOIN THE CLUB

These operations cater primarily to small businesses and "qualified" individuals. To become an individual member, the applicant usually must belong to a particular group, such as a credit union, saver's club, investor's club, government employee's group, community association, utility company employee, senior citizen, etc. As you can see, individual qualifications are written so broadly that it would be hard for an individual not to be able to qualify.

The major players in this market are Price Club, Sam's Wholesale, Costco and PACE. Others (at this writing) include BJ's Wholesale Club, Price Savers, The Wholesale Club, and Warehouse Club. Cities in which these clubs presently operate are shown below. New stores are being added at a rapid clip, so if your town isn't shown, you may want to check with the home office of one or more of the discounter's (or your local Chamber of Commerce) to find out if one is planned for your area in the near future.

WHO AND WHERE THEY ARE

BJ's Wholesale Club Inc., One Mercer Road, P. O. Box 3000, Natick, MA 01760. Tel. (617) 651-7400. Membership fees: Business $25.00 annual, individual $25.00 annual.

Warehouses: **Connecticut:** Hartford. **Delaware:** New Castle. **Florida:** Hialeah Gardens, Miami, Sunrise. **Illinois:** Calumet City, Hillside, Niles, Rolling Meadows. **Massachusetts:** Chicopee, Medford, Westboro, Weymouth, North Dartmouth. **New Hampshire:** Salem. **New Jersey:** Maple Shade. **New York:** Albany, Buffalo, East Farmingdale, East Rutherford, North Syracuse, Rochester. **Ohio:** Toledo. **Pennsylvania:** Camp Hill, Philadelphia. **Rhode Island:** Johnston. **Virginia:** Virginia Beach.

Merchandise: Deli, bakery, baking supplies, tobacco, fish, meat, paper, household supplies, canned & frozen foods, spices, tea & coffee, dairy, pet food & supplies, grocery items, health & beauty aids, housewares, soft goods, clocks & watches, books, auto supplies, electronics, office supplies, hardware, small appliances, sporting goods, batteries, film & film processing.

COSTCO Wholesale Corporation, 10809 120th Avenue NE, Kirkland, WA 98033. Tel. (206) 828-8100. Membership fees: Business $25.00 annual, individual $30.00 annual.

Warehouses: **Alaska:** Anchorage. **California:** Bakersfield, Canoga Park, City of Industry, Clovis, Danville, Fremont,

Fresno, Garden Grove, Hawthorne, Lancaster, Martinez, Modesto, Richmond, Riverside, San Bernardino, San Bruno, Sand City, San Jose, San Leandro, Santa Clara, Santa Maria, Santa Rosa, Stockton, Vallejo, Van Nuys, Victorville, Visalia. **Florida:** Clearwater, Davie, Fort Lauderdale, Kendall, Lauderhill, Miami, Orlando, Palm Beach Gardens, Palm Harbor, Pompano Beach, South Orlando, Tampa, West Palm Beach. **Hawaii:** Honolulu. **Idaho:** Boise. **Massachusetts:** Danvers, West Springfield. **Nevada:** Las Vegas, Reno. **Oregon:** Aloha, Clackamas, Eugene, Portland, Tulatin. **Utah:** Salt Lake City. **Washington:** Federal Way, Kenneywick, Kirkland, Lynwood, Seattle, Silverdale, Spokane, Tacoma, Tuykwila, Union Gap. **CANADA: Alberta:** Calgary, Edmonton. **British Columbia:** Burnaby, Richmond, Surrey. **Ontario:** Winnepeg.

Merchandise: Apparel, audio & video tapes, beer & wine, books, calculators, cameras, candy, cigarettes, computer supplies, deli products, domestics, drug store items, frozen foods, furniture, giftware, groceries, hardware, housewares, janitorial supplies, jewelry & watches, appliances, meat products, office equipment & supplies, perishables, photo processing, sporting goods, stereos, sundries, supermarket items, televisions, tires & automotive, tools, toys, typewriters.

Home Club, 140 Orangefair Mall, Suite 100, Fullerton, CA 92632. Tel. (714) 441-0171. Members previously received 5% lower prices than non-members, but this policy has been changed. All shoppers now receive the same prices.

Warehouses: **California:** Canoga Park, Chula Vista, El Cajon, El Monte, Fountain Valle˜ Fullerton, Gardena, Glendora, Hawaiian Gardens, Industry, Inglewood, Irvine, Ladera Heights, Laguna Niguel, Montclair, Moreno Valley, North Hollywood, Norwalk, Riverside, San Bernardino, San Marcos, Stanton.

Merchandise: Building materials & supplies of all kinds, chemicals, electrical goods, furniture, garden tools & supplies, hand tools, hardware, household accessories, household appliances, lighting fixtures, painting supplies, plumbing materials, pool supplies.

The Home Depot, 2727 Paces Ferry Road, Atlanta, GA 30339. Tel. (404) 433-8211. Not a membership organization.

Warehouses: **Alabama:** Mobile, Huntsville. **Arizona:** *Phoenix area* - Camelback, Cave Creek, Covina, Glendale, Mesa, Scottsdale, Tempe, Thomas Road; *Tucson area* — East Broadway, Oracle Road. **California:** *Southern* — Cerritos, Chula Vista, City of Industry, Corona, El Cajon, Escondido, Fullerton, Gardena, Huntington Beach, La Mirada, Monrovia, Oceanside, Oxnard, Long Beach, Pico Rivera, San Bernardino, San Diego (3), San Fernando, Santee, Tustin, Upland, Van Nuys; *Northern* - Carmichael, Colma, Fremont, Milpitas, San Carlos, San Jose, San Leandro, Sunnyvale. **Connecticut**: Berlin, North Haven. **Florida:** *Southern* — Davie, Deerfield Beach, Dixie Highway, Flagler, Hialeah, Fort Myers, Hollywood, Jensen Beach, Kendall, Lake Park, Lauderdale Lakes, Margate, North Miami Beach, Palm Springs; *Northern* — Atlantic, Blanding, Gainesville, Ramona; *Central* — Altamonte Springs, Colonial Drive, Daytona, Melbourne, Southland Blvd, W. Colonial Drive; *Tampa Bay area* — Brandon, Clearwater, Hillsborough, Largo, Port Richey, St. Petersburg, Sarasota, Tampa. **Georgia**: Buckhead, Decatur, Doraville, Douglasville, Duluth, Forest Park, Kennesaw, Marietta, Roswell. **Louisiana**: Baton Rouge, East New Orleans, Gretna, Harahan, Shreveport. **New Jersey**: East Hannover. **New York**: *Long Island* — East Meadow, Patchogue. **South Carolina**: Greenville, Spartanburg. **Tennessee**: Antioch, Chattanooga, Knoxville, Madison. **Texas:** *Dallas/Ft. Worth area*: Arlington, Carrollton, Forest Lane, Mesquite, North Richland Hills, Northwest Highway, Plano, Richardson, Westmoreland, White Settlement; *Houston area* — Bellerive, FM 1960, Gulf Freeway, Lumpkin, Market Street, Stuebner.

Merchandise: Each warehouse carries approximately 30,000 building and home supply items consisting of hardware, lighting, lumber, plumbing equipment & supplies, tools, etc. In addition to an exceptionally large inventory, this chain is noted for its knowledgeable sales people.

Pace Membership Warehouse, 3350 Peoria Street, Aurora, CO 80010. Tel. (303) 364-0700. Memberships: Business $25.00 annual, individual $25.00 annual.

Warehouses: **California**: Cathedral City, Chino, Downey, El Monte, Fountain Valley, Fullerton, Gardena, San Bernardino, San Fernando, Woodland Hills. **Colorado**: Arvada, Aurora, Colorado Springs, Fort Collins, Sheridan. **Connecticut**: Berlin. **Florida**: Hillsborough County, Palm Harbor, Pinellas Park, Tampa. **Georgia**: Forest Park, Marietta, Norcross, Roswell, Stone Mountain. **Iowa**: Des Moines. **Kentucky**: Lexington, Louisville. **Maryland**: Baltimore (2), Capitol Heights, Landover, Laurel. **Michigan:** Farmington Hills, Flint, Kalamazoo, Madison Heights, Roseville, Saginaw, Taylor, Westland, Ypsilanti. **Nebraska:** Omaha. **New York**: Cheektowaga. **North Carolina:** Cary, Charlotte (2), Greensboro. **Ohio:** Cincinnati, Cleveland (2), Toledo. **Pennsylvania**: Hatboro, Langhorne, Monroeville, Ross Township, West Miffin. **Rhode Island:** Warwick.

Merchandise: Office equipment & supplies, fresh produce, furniture, tires & auto supplies, Tvs, VCRs, stereos, jewelry & watches, clothing, linens, groceries & frozen foods, tobacco products, sundries, hardware, housewares, janitorial supplies, appliances, health & beauty aids, sporting goods, toys, books.

Price Club, 2647 Arianne, San Diego, CA 92117. Tel. (619) 581-4600. Memberships: Business $25.00 annual, individual $25.00 annual.

Warehouses: **Arizona:** Glendale, Mesa, Phoenix, Scottsdale, Tempe, Tucson (2). **California:** Alhambra, Azusa, Bakersfield, Burbank, Chula Vista, Coachella Valley, Colton, Concord, Corona, Fountain Valley, Fullerton, Hayward, Inglewood, North Highlands, Northridge, Norwalk, Oxnard, Pomona, Rancho Cordova, Rancho Mirage, Redwood City, Richmond, Sacramento, San Diego (2), San Jose, San Juan Capistrano, San

Marcos, Santee, Signal Hill, South San Francisco, Sunnyvale. **Colorado:** Aurora, Westminster. **Connecticut:** North Haven. **Maryland:** Gaithersburg, Glen Burnie, Baltimore, Beltsville, Suitland. **New Jersey:** Edison, Mapleshade. **New Mexico:** Albuquerque. **New York:** Cheektowaga, Copiague, Smithtown. **Virginia:** Fairfax, Hampton, Loudoun, Norfolk, Richmond, South Richmond.

Merchandise: Office equipment & supplies, restaurant supplies, computer supplies, typewriters, calculators, tools, janitorial supplies, food, frozen food, perishables, wine, spirits, sundries, books, jewelry, appliances, housewares, giftware, clothing, automotive supplies, tires, sporting goods.

Price Savers Wholesale Warehouse, 986 Atherton Drive, Suite 220, Salt Lake City, UT 84123. Tel. 1-801-466-7777. Memberships: Company $25.00 annual; individual - no fee but prices are 5% higher than member's unless individual buys a PlusCard for a $30.00 annual fee.

Warehouses: **Alaska:** Anchorage. **Arizona:** Gilbert, Phoenix (3). **California:** City of Industry, Irvine, Montclair, Rancho Cordova, Sacramento, South Gate, Stanton. **Utah:** Murray, Ogden, Provo, Salt Lake City. **Washington:** Fife, Seattle.

Merchandise: frozen foods, deli, dairy products, bakery items, snacks, produce, spirits, condiments, office supplies & furniture, computers, typewriters, calculators, entertainment centers, lamps, paper, cleaning supplies, vacuums, household supplies, electronics, appliances, hardware, tools, health & sports equipment, and automotive supplies.

Sam's Wholesale Club, c/o Wal-Mart Stores Inc., Bentonville, AR 72712. Tel. (501) 273-4000. Membership: Company $25.00 annual.

Warehouses: **Alabama**: Birmingham, Huntsville, Irondale, Mobile, Montgomery. **Arkansas:** Little Rock, Fort Smith, North Little Rock, Springdale. **Colorado:** Colorado Springs, Loveland. **Florida:** Daytona Beach, Fern Park, Fort Myers, Fort Pierce, Gainesville, Jacksonville (2), Lakeland, Lantana,

Melbourne, Orlando, Panama City, Pensacola, Sarasota, Tallahassee. **Georgia:** Atlanta, Augusta, Austell, Columbus, Duluth, Macon, Marietta, Savannah. **Illinois:** Joliet, Naperville, Peoria, Streamwood, Matteson, Springfield, O'Fallon, Rockford. **Indiana:** Evansville, Fishers, Goshen, Lafayette, Merrillville, Terre Haute. **Iowa:** Cedar Rapids, Davenport. **Kansas:** Lenexa, Wichita. **Kentucky:** Florence, Jeffersontown. Louisville. **Louisiana:** Baton Rouge, Harvey, Kenner, Lake Charles, Monroe, New Orleans, Scott, Shreveport (2). **Michigan:** Flint, Lansing. **Mississippi:** Gulfport, Jackson. **Missouri:** Columbia, Ferguson, Grandview, Kansas City (2), Springfield, St. Charles, St. Louis. **Nebraska:** Omaha. **New Jersey:** Atlantic City, Delran Township. **North Carolina:** Fayetteville, Matthews, Raleigh, Wilmington, Winston-Salem. **North Dakota:** Fargo. **Ohio:** Cincinnati (2), Dayton, Holland. **Oklahoma:** Lawton, Midwest City, Oklahoma City (2), Tulsa. **Pennsylvania:** Temple, York. **South Carolina:** Columbia, Greenville, North Charleston, Spartanburg. **South Dakota:** Sioux Falls. **Tennessee:** Chattanooga, Kingsport, Knoxville, Memphis (2), Nashville (2). **Texas:** Abilene, Amarillo, Austin (2), Beaumont, Brownsville, Corpus Christi, Dallas (3), El Paso (2), Fort Worth, Grand Prairie, Houston (5), Laredo, Lubbock, Meadows, Midland, Pharr, Plano, Richland Hills, San Antonio (3), Texarkana, Tyler, Waco, White Settlement, Wichita Falls. **Virginia:** Roanoke. **West Virginia:** Cross Lanes. **Wisconsin:** Brookfield, Franklin, Green Bay, Madison.

Merchandise: Office supplies, computer equipment, food products, frozen foods, tires & batteries, auto supplies, televisions, camcorders, VCRs, major appliances, small appliances, home furnishings, designer clothing, sheets & towels, small building equipment, hardware, candy, snack items, watches & jewelry.

Warehouse Club, 7235 N. Linder Avenue, Skokie, IL 60077. Tel. (708) 679-6800. Memberships: Business $25.00 annual, individual $35.00, or individuals may elect to pay 5% higher prices instead of membership fee.

Warehouses: **Illinois**:   Bridgeview, Niles.   **Indiana:**
Hammond.   **Michigan:**   Allen Park, Hazel Park, Redford
Township.   **Ohio:**   Akron,   Columbus   (2),   Dayton.
Pennsylvania: Bridgeville, North Versailles.

Merchandise: Apparel, linens, office supplies, furniture,
appliances, tools, automotive supplies, electronics, video and
audio tapes, snack foods, health & beauty aids, tobacco,
alcoholic beverages, soft drinks, household supplies, groceries,
seasonal items.

The Wholesale Club, 7260 Shadeland Station, Indianapolis, IN
46256.   Tel. (317) 842-0351 or (317) 842-0351, ext. 111 for
membership information.   Membership: Business $25.00
annual.

Warehouses: **Indiana:** Carmel, Fort Wayne, Greenwood,
Indianapolis   (2),   South   Bend/Mishawaka.   **Michigan:**
Kentwood,   Portage.   **Minnesota**:   Burnsville, Fridley,
Hermantown, Inver Grove Heights, St. Louis Park, White Bear
Lake. **Ohio:** Bedford, Boardman, Brook Park, Columbus (2),
Eastlake, Elyria/Lorain, Niles,   North Canton. **Wisconsin**:
Grand Chute, Menomonee Falls, West Allis.

Merchandise: Apparel, beverages, books, calculators, cheese
& dairy, film, frozen foods, hardware & tools, health & beauty
aids, home furnishings, housewares, institutional foods, janitorial
supplies, jewelry, luggage, major appliances, microwaves, office
furniture & supplies, photo processing, sporting goods, stereo &
CD players.

DISCOUNT CHAINS

Discount chains (also known as full-line discounters) such as
K-Mart, Target and Wal-Mart, are still the sales volume leader
in the discount sales market place. They sell merchandise at
lower prices than many retailers, but usually not as low as
warehouse clubs or as some of the buying services listed
elsewhere in this report. Warehouse clubs and buying services
often offer better buys—either lower prices on the same goods or

better quality products at equal prices—than the full line discounters.

The discount chains continue to prosper and grow, however. They have broader geographic coverage than warehouses (at least at present) and many of them carry wider ranges of merchandise and more selection in the lines they do carry.

Discount chains have far too many store locations to list in this report, and most readers will be familiar with those in their area anyway. If not, they can be found in the yellow pages under Department Stores. Some of the general merchandisers in this market are **Ames, Bradlees, Caldor, Hills, Consolidated Stores, K-Mart, Meijer, Mervyn's, Fred Myer, Rose's, ShopKo, Target, and Wal-Mart.**

SPECIALTY DISCOUNTERS

Major specialty discount retailers include **Bill's Dollar Stores, Circuit City** (electronics), **Clothestime** (apparel), **Dollar General, Dress Barn** (apparel), **Family Dollar, Hit or Miss** (apparel), **Kay-Bee** (toys), **Marshalls** (apparel), **T. J. Maxx** (apparel), **Toys "R" Us** (toys).

Chapter 22

U. S. GOVERNMENT PROPERTY

One of the largest purveyors of properties in the United States is the U. S. Government. Items sold by Uncle Sam include every conceivable type of merchandise: automobiles and other vehicles, houses, boats, airplanes, jewelry, office equipment, machine tools, land, real estate, and an almost endless list of other items.

Some of these goods are property which has become surplus to the government's needs, some are items which have been seized by law enforcement officials in drug raids or by the IRS for delinquent taxes. Much of the real property has been taken over by the Government as a result of the great Savings & Loan disaster and turned over to the newly created Resolution Trust Corporation for disposal.

BARGAINS FROM UNCLE SAM

In this cornucopia of vehicles, equipment, land, and buildings there are bargains to be had. This is not to say that every item is sold at a fraction of its value. The people in charge of disposing of this great residue of purchases made with taxpayer's money (or seized for cause) are responsible for getting the highest price possible. Sometimes, though, the highest price is still a bargain compared to what you would pay elsewhere. It all depends on how many people are competing for the item—and how well they have done their market research.

MARKETING METHODS

With the possible exception of real properties taken over by the Resolution Trust Corporation (RTC), most items sold by the Government are sold at public auction. At this writing, the RTC seemed in a muddle as to how it is going to proceed with the tens of thousands of real estate holdings in its hands. It was reportedly still looking for real estate agents across the country to assist it in the massive undertaking of unloading the fruits of the S&L follies.

After you obtain information on the goods for sale from one of the sources listed in the following paragraphs, we suggest that you re-read Chapter 17 on Auctions before jumping into the auction fray.

SALES AGENCIES

The U. S. General Services Administration (GSA) is the principal agency for selling Federal personal property of civilian agencies, although the U.S. Marshals Service oversees disposal of some property seized by Government agencies. The Bureau of Land Management (BLM) has jurisdiction over disposal of surplus undeveloped Government land (except that coming under the RTC). The Department of Defense (DoD) sells its own surplus property.

Drug enforcement agencies handle sales of items seized in drug related cases because of a law which permits them to use the proceeds of such sales in running their respective departments. Most of this property is turned over to public auction houses for the actual sale. However, sometimes these agencies ask the GSA to handle such sales for them. As mentioned above, the Resolution Trust Corporation (RTC) is responsible for selling off real estate of all sorts in connection with the S&L fiasco.

GENERAL SERVICES ADMINISTRATION

For more detailed information on GSA sales, and to get on their mailing list for notification of upcoming auctions in your area, contact the appropriate office listed below:

National Capital Region: *Washington D.C. and nearby Maryland and Virginia*. General Services Administration, 7th and D Streets, Washington, DC 20407.

Region 1: *Connecticut, Maine, Massachusetts, New Hampshire, Rhode Island, and Vermont.* General Services Administration, Post Office and Courthouse, Boston, MA 02109.

Region 2: *New Jersey, New York, Puerto Rico, and Virgin Islands.* General Services Administration, 26 Federal Plaza, New York, NY 10278.

Region 3: *Delaware, Maryland, Virginia, Pennsylvania, and West Virginia.* General Services Administration, Ninth and Market Streets, Philadelphia, PA 19107.

Region 4: *Alabama, Florida, Georgia, Kentucky, Mississippi, North Carolina, South Carolina, and Tennessee.* General Services Administration, 75 Spring St SW, Atlanta, GA 30303.

Region 5: *Illinois, Indiana, Michigan, Minnesota, Ohio, and Wisconsin.* General Services Administration, 230 S. Dearborn Street, Chicago, IL 60604.

Region 6: *Iowa, Kansas, Missouri and Nebraska*, General Services Administration, 1500 E. Bannister Road, Kansas City, MO 64132.

Region 7: *Arkansas, Louisiana, New Mexico, Oklahoma, and Texas.* General Services Administration, 819 Tyler Street, Fort Worth, TX 76102.

Region 8: *Colorado, Montana, North Dakota, South Dakota, Utah, and Wyoming.* General Services Administration, Building 41 - Denver Federal Center, Denver, CO 80225.

Region 9: *Arizona, California, Northern Mariana Islands, Guam, Hawaii, and Nevada*: General Services Administration, 525 Market Street, San Francisco, CA 94105.

Region 10: *Alaska, Idaho, Oregon and Washington.* General Services Administration, GSA Center, Auburn, WA 98002.

U. S. MARSHALS SERVICE

For information on upcoming auctions, watch for announcements in *USA Today* on the third Wednesday of each month, or call their headquarters at (202) 307-9221.

BUREAU OF LAND MANAGEMENT

For information on undeveloped land available from the Bureau of Land Management, write and ask for their brochure *Are There Any Public Lands For Sale?* This brochure provides useful information on this subject, and lists the addresses of the various state offices which can be contacted for property listings in each area. Write to: **U. S. Department of The Interior, Bureau of Land Management**, Washington, DC 20240.

Adopt an Animal Program: The BLM also operates an adoption program for wild horses and burros. These are animals removed from public lands in order to prevent over-population. Prices range from $75 for burros to $125 for horses. Buyers have to agree to be responsible for proper corralling, feeding and health maintenance of the animals. For information on this program, telephone (916) 978-4725.

DEPARTMENT OF DEFENSE

Surplus items sold by DoD include such items as aircraft components, accessories, and equipment; ships, small craft, pontoons, & floating docks; ship and marine equipment; railway equipment; motor vehicles, trailers and cycles; tractors, engines, woodworking equipment, hardware, electrical equipment, office equipment, and hundreds of other items.

Most property is sold at auction. However, negotiated sales are authorized in some cases (e.g., when acceptable bids have not been received). Retail sales are conducted at some locations and offer small quantities of individual items at fixed prices.

Some DoD property is available by catalog. To receive a copy, write to **DRMR Headquarters**, 74 N. Washington, Battle Creek, MI 49017.

DoD has several marketing region sales offices (known as **Defense Reutilization and Marketing Regions, or DRMR's**). Each sales office conducts sales of property held by installations within a given geographical area. This includes preparation of sales catalogs, conducting bids, and concluding contractual arrangements. Upon request, a sales office will provide the locations of the installations in its geographical area where property is located. Following are the addresses of these sales offices:

DRMR - Columbus, P. O. Box 500, Blacklick, OH 43004-0500, Telephone (614) 238-2114.

DRMR - Memphis, P. O. Box 14716, Memphis, TN 38114-0716, Telephone (901) 775-6417.

DRMR - Ogden, P. O. Box 53, Defense Depot Ogden, Ogden, UT 84407-5001, Telephone (801) 399-7257.

DRMR - Hawaii, Box 211, Pearl City, HI 96782-0211, Telephone (805) 455-5158.

DRMR - Europe, APO NY 09633, Telephone 06121-82-3505.

DRMR - Australia, FPO San Francisco 96680-2920, Telephone 099-49-3214.

Additional Information: For more information, including details on methods of sale and getting on bidders lists, write and request a copy of the publication *How To Buy Surplus Personal Property From The United States Department of Defense*. Send your request and a check or money order for $1.50 to **U. S. Government Printing Office**, Superintendent of Documents, Washington, DC 20402.

RESOLUTION TRUST CORPORATION

As of this writing, the United States Government has more than 30,000 properties valued at over *$160 BILLION dollars* and the list continues to grow with every S&L that goes belly up. The Resolution Trust Corporation was established by Congress to dispose of the properties acquired in the bailout of failed S&L's. Perhaps by the time this report comes off the press, the RTC will have come up with a scheme for marketing these properties.

The RTC is supposed to sell its real estate holdings at or near fair market value. However, pressure is building—and will no doubt increase—for it to start unloading these properties in order to bring in cash to help offset the horrendous cost of this massive bailout. For example, just as this book was going to press the RTC had just completed an auction of 1100 properties in Texas (using the auction firm of Kennedy-Wilson Inc. of Santa Monica, California). These 1100 properties brought a total of $12.2 million to Uncle Sam—about $11,000 per property on average. Officials refused to say what the properties were valued at, but you can bet their original cost was several times the selling price. Look for more tremendous bargains to develop on RTC holdings as time goes on.

More Information: Catalogs listing RTC properties are available in four categories—**Land; Commercial; Residential (single family); and Residential (multi-family).** Each catalog covers properties nationwide, and is broken down by state and city. Catalogs for land or commercial properties sell for $10.00 each, and those for residential properties are $15.00 each.

Catalogs may be ordered from the RTC at the following address: **Resolution Trust Corporation,** P. O. Box 539002, Grand Prairie, TX 75053, telephone (800) 431-0600. Orders by telephone must be paid by Master Card or Visa. Mail orders may be paid by check.

Chapter 23

OFFBEAT BARGAIN OPPORTUNITIES

Outside the more sophisticated world of direct mail, electronic shopping, warehouse clubs, and auctions, bargain opportunities may exist in your own neighborhood. Those with time to browse and a good nose for good buys will enjoy checking out one or more of the following sources.

CONSIGNMENT SHOPS

These establishments act as "stocking" brokers for owners of used furniture and other household articles. Some of them handle other items as well. Sellers use these outlets because they feel they can get more for their goods via this market, or because they like the convenience of having someone else do their selling.

Knowledgeable buyers can often find items in excellent condition at attractive prices in these shops. They usually offer at one location a larger variety of a given item than can be found at a garage or lawn sale, saving the time and expense of running from one garage sale to another.

How They Work: Consignment houses and the seller normally agree on an initial asking price. The price is fixed for a set period of time, usually 30 days. At the end of that time, the shop typically has the right to lower the price, say by 10%. The new price will be in effect for 30 days more unless the article is sold. At the end of that time, the contract may provide that the price can again be reduced by a set percentage. If it has not sold at the end of the extended period, either a new contract will be negotiated, the article will be returned to the seller, or it will be "donated" to the shop which may then dispose of it in any way it sees fit.

The shop takes a percentage of the ultimate selling price as its sales commission. The percentage may vary, depending on the sales price established for the article being sold. Commissions of 50% on items selling for up to one hundred dollars, and 30% to 35% on more expensive items, are typical examples.

To know whether an item is or is not a bargain, you should (a) know the price of a similar new item, and (b) shop around at other consignment shops for comparative prices. If the initial price is too high to suit you, you can wait for it to be reduced and hope that it is still around when the initial time period expires.

Consignment shops may be found in the telephone yellow pages under Consignment Shops, Consignment Services, or Consignment Stores.

GARAGE SALES

This seemingly mundane neighborhood market place can be the source of household and garden items perfectly suitable for their purpose, and obtainable at a fraction of new price. A used shovel, rake, frying pan, bicycle, book, or whatever may serve the buyer every bit as well as a new one.

Garage sales may be located by watching for neighborhood signs, supermarket bulletin boards, signs in shop windows, or ads in local newspapers or shopping throw-aways.

Hidden Treasures: In addition to the usual run of used household articles, second-hand clothes and sundry junk, garage sales can sometimes turn up the equivalent of "hidden treasure." One of the hot *avocation cum vocation* activities being practiced by an increasing number of shoppers at garage sales, consignment shops and swap meets is the pursuit of collectibles. A collectible, for want of a better definition, might be called one man's junk and another man's treasure. It is an article that is no longer made and is now in relatively short supply. It may not have been very valuable at the time it was current (e.g. old beer bottles, used smoking pipes, 78 rpm phonographs, etc.), but now fetches ten or a hundred times its original value.

For more on this subject, including 350 pages of what collectors want to buy and the names, addresses and phone numbers of buyers, you can check at your local library for the book *Cash For Your Undiscovered Treasures*, by Tony Hyman. If it is not available there, and/or if you would like to own it, the book may be ordered from Buyer Directory, Box 699, Claremont, CA 91711 for $19.95 plus $3.00 shipping.

SWAP MEETS

In the past 30 years swap meets have gone from small neighborhood operations known as flea markets to big business in large outdoor or indoor arenas that cater to thousands of bargain hunters. There are dozens of these fairs located from coast to coast, most of which are open only on weekends. Probably the nation's largest is Trader's Village, located between Dallas and Fort Worth, Texas. It fills over 100 acres and provides space for 1200 vendors.

What They Sell: In the past goods sold at these bazaars were mostly hand-crafted articles, used items from someone's attic, or damaged goods being disposed of at cut rate prices. In recent years, however, the mix of goods being offered has shifted more to new merchandise.

Whether new or used, there is no end to the variety of goods offered at swap meets. Items from Abacuses to Zithers—and everything in between—may be found on any given weekend at the modern meet. On rare occasions, valuable collectibles may be found at swap meets (see the preceding comments under garage sales).

Where They Are: To locate swap meets in your area, look in the yellow pages under "Swap Meets and Shops," look through the ads in the local newspaper, or check with the administrator of your local fairgrounds or college. Meets require a large outdoor space, so fairgrounds and college parking lots are prime locations—and officials like the extra revenue brought in by otherwise idle assets!

Buyer Beware: Shoppers at swap meets should be wary of counterfeit merchandise. These meets are prime marketing spots for sellers of bogus goods because the vendors assume that most meet shoppers are suckers for a bargain, even if the "bargain" is too good to be true.

There seem to be counterfeiters for almost anything for which there is a market, but items currently being counterfeited in great quantities include electrical appliances, auto parts, computer software, audio & video tapes, clothing, tools, and watches—especially the more expensive variety.

Chapter 24

JUST ABOUT EVERYTHING IS NEGOTIABLE

In most cultures outside the United States, bargaining between seller and buyer is not only accepted, it is expected. In the souks of North Africa and the Middle East, in the bazaars of Asia, in the tourist shops in Latin America and elsewhere, negotiating the price of an item is an integral part of the ritual—and the enjoyment—in making the deal. Indeed, the satisfaction derived by both purchaser and seller in the negotiating process is probably as great as that obtained in making the deal.

Some degree of negotiation takes place in this country on major purchases such as homes and automobiles, and a few savvy people have learned that other goods are also susceptible to this process. However, most people are inclined to accept the first price quoted by the vendor as gospel. This is a mistake, if you truly want to save money.

To become really effective at getting good value for money spent, i.e., to reach your goal of improving your standard of living by making your present income go farther than it presently does, it is important that you realize that literally *just about everything* is negotiable!

You don't need a college degree in psychology or labor relations to become an effective negotiator. All you need to do is learn some basic rules and apply them.

REMEMBER THE OBJECTIVES

Your Objective: When you enter into negotiations with a potential seller, you are doing so with a particular aim in mind—you want to buy the article in question at a price acceptable to you. To reach this goal, be prepared to take the time necessary to negotiate patiently with the other party until success is achieved—or until you become convinced that a deal is not possible.

The Seller's Objective: The vendor wants to make the sale to you just as badly as you want to make the purchase and in many cases, more so. This is true for the simple reason that you, as customer, usually have other vendors you can go to if you don't get the deal you want, whereas the seller—although he may have other potential customers—has irretrievably lost one sale if you walk out the door. Keeping this fact in mind puts you in a stronger bargaining position than the seller.

BE PREPARED

You are not ready to begin negotiations until you have collected as much market information as possible. An unknown businessman is quoted as having said "you never have all the information you need to make a good business decision, but you sure better have all you can get." This admonition applies equally well to our personal business.

Before attempting to negotiate with the potential seller, it is important that you know (1) what you want, (2) the going market rate for the item, and (3) the maximum amount you are willing to pay for it.

NEGOTIATE WITH THE RIGHT PERSON

Determine at the outset whether the sales person you are dealing with has the authority to enter into price negotiations with you. You can do this by simply saying "I'm interested in possibly buying XYZ from you, provided we can come to terms. Are you authorized to discuss price with me?" It is frustrating to spend time and effort negotiating only to find out that the salesperson you have been talking with doesn't have the authority to make a deal.

If the salesperson tells you he/she is not authorized to deviate from the published price, or that the price is not negotiable, tell him you want to speak with his superior, or the department manager, or whoever is next up the ladder. Chances are that this next person will be empowered to negotiate with you. However, if he also tells you that the published price is firm, politely tell him you are sorry because you would have liked to have done business with his establishment, then leave.

WATCH YOUR DEMEANOR

Remember, the sole purpose of your discussion is to try to conclude a business arrangement of benefit to both of you. If you have done your homework on the current market, and know the maximum price you are prepared to pay, you are in position to play your hand in a calm, business-like manner. While wild outbursts, chest-pounding and hand-wringing is considered normal in certain foreign market places, they are not welcomed and usually are not effective in the good old USA. Rather, the person who stays the coolest is most apt to prevail in the end.

KEEP SOMETHING IN RESERVE

Don't play all your cards at once. For example, suppose you have decided to buy a new television set and a VCR, you have decided on the brands and models you want, you have made a study of the market and know the going prices for each, and are now ready to start dickering with a sales representative. Start off by offering a price for the TV set several dollars below what you have already decided your maximum price will be.

After a period of serious negotiating, you decide that you have just about got the salesman's lowest offer. At this point, you say "Jack, that is still more money than I am willing to pay for that set. But, I'm also interested in a (brand and model) VCR which you carry. Tell you what I'll do, I'll give you X dollars for the two of them." This not only keeps the negotiating process alive, it hones the appetite of the sales person because he now sees the possibility of two sales instead of one. If he is working on commission (or against a sales quota), you have suddenly given him a little larger window of opportunity, and made it possible for him to be more flexible than before.

REFUSE TO BE RUSHED

The person who controls the pace of the negotiation usually controls the outcome. For that reason, many sales people will attempt to hurry you into making a deal. Don't let this tactic succeed. Keep asking questions and negotiating until you have received an offer that is acceptable to you, or have decided that no deal is possible. This strategy does several things in your behalf: It keeps the negotiations alive, the answers to your questions provides you with additional information which might come in handy in making further points, and it causes the other party to invest additional time, energy, and personal involvement in the proceedings. The more investment he has made in the situation, the more difficult it is for him to abandon it without making a strong attempt to salvage the sale.

KNOW WHEN TO WALK AWAY

There will be times when you have followed all the rules and done the best job of negotiating possible, without apparent success. Unless the item for which you have been negotiating is the only one of it's kind in the world and you absolutely must have it *now* no matter what, it is time to apply the next to last rule in the game of negotiating. Say politely to the other party, "I'm sorry. I would have liked to buy XYZ from you, but it looks as if I will have to go elsewhere. Thank you for your interest and your time." Then start to leave.

One of three things will happen: The salesman will: (1) stop you before you get out the door and accept your final offer; (2) walk with you towards the door while continuing to negotiate; or, (3) let you depart. In the first instance you have succeeded, in the second you still have a chance of succeeding, and in the third you have the opportunity of going to another vendor where you might succeed.

In the event you do not make a deal, leave your name and telephone number with the salesman. Don't be surprised if he calls you within 24 hours in an attempt to salvage the sale. This is especially true if your positions were fairly close when discussions were terminated. Even after walking away, you may still succeed.

THE FINAL RULE

The last rule in negotiating, whether or not you were successful, is to always end on a friendly note. First, this may have a bearing on whether the salesman thinks things over and calls you later to accept your offer. Second, you may find that you are unable to get as good a deal elsewhere as you were offered here and decide to return. Third, you may want to negotiate a future purchase of some other item with this firm, in which case it's much better to be remembered as a pleasant individual than as a cantankerous old goat.

Chapter 25

SPECIAL DEALS FOR SENIOR CITIZENS

People in the United States aged 50 and over are in a class by themselves when it comes to money saving opportunities. They can not only take advantage of the many suggestions contained elsewhere in this volume, but as a group they qualify for special deals not available to the under-50 crowd.

An ever increasing number of business organizations are catering to seniors. A few important (and impressive) statistics will explain why. In the U.S. the over-50 group:

[1] Makes up slightly over 25% of the population,

[2] Is the fastest growing age group in the country,

[3] Has the highest per-capita income,

[4] Earns over 1/2 of the total discretionary income,

[5] Has twice the discretionary income of under 35's,

[6] Controls 70% of net worth of all households.

Members of this group are being wooed with discounts, premiums, prizes, and other special deals not because of their age or good looks but because of their spending power. But never mind the reason why. If you belong to this elite buying class, make the most of it.

WHO QUALIFIES?

The rest of this chapter will be devoted to special deals just for you. But first, a caveat or two. The age at which a person qualifies as a senior may be 50, 55, 60, 62, or 65—it all depends on the policy of the organization with which you are dealing. Some businesses require that you be a member of the American

Association of Retired Persons (AARP), or similar organization, and show your membership card. Others will ask for a driver's license or other ID to prove your age.

GET ALL THE DETAILS

Whether you are dealing with a hotel, restaurant, fast food chain, airline, tour group, movie theater or whatever, **always ask** if they have a discount program for senior citizens. Many of them who have such a program don't advertise it and won't mention it unless you inquire.

Ask about the full range of discounts available. Some special deals are available only to members of one or more seniors organizations. (Information on the more prominent seniors groups is given later in this chapter). Remember, though, that you may have a membership in another organization such as an auto club, veteran's group, or some other entity which qualifies you for a better discount than that afforded seniors. It pays to compare.

Following is a listing of some of the special deals just for you, together with tips on where to get information on others.

AIRLINE FARES

Chapter 11 covered the wide range of fares—and potential savings—available to all travelers. Following are some special deals which are available to Senior Citizens only.

Domestic Airlines: Nine of the major airlines allow a 10% discount off their published fares, including advance-purchase super-savers, for senior citizens. For those aged 62 or over, eight airlines offer flight coupon books. These represent one of the best deals around for seniors. They are available from **Alaska, American, America West, Continental, Delta, Eastern, Northwest, TWA, United and USAir.**

Coupon books can be bought with four or eight coupons. Each coupon represents one ticket. Prices range from $384 to

$464 per book of four, and from $598 to $776 for a book of eight at the time of this writing.

On Continental, Delta, Northwest and USAir, one coupon is good between any two points in the continental US served by that particular airline, even if stops or plane changes are involved. Other lines have mileage caps per coupon (typically 2000 miles). Almost all of them contain restrictions of one sort or another. The programs vary from one airline to another, so be sure and ask for details when inquiring about these specials.

Foreign Airlines: The following foreign airlines offer special deals of one kind or another to seniors. Qualification requirements—and restrictions—vary widely, so check directly with the airline or with your travel agent for complete details in each case: **Air Canada, British Airways, El Al, Finnair, KLM, TAP Air Portugal,** and **SAS.**

AUTO RENTALS

The following auto rental firms offer special rates to seniors: **Alamo, American International, Avis, Budget, Dollar, General, Hertz, National, Thrifty.** Most of them require that you be a member of AARP or some other recognized senior citizens organization.

Rates and discounts vary, and in some cases may not be as good as you can get through some other arrangement (e.g., membership in AAA or another organization, corporate rates, etc.), so check all possibilities before renting.

BANKS

The financial statistics associated with the senior group, as outlined in the opening paragraphs of this chapter, have not escaped the attention of banks and savings institutions—those folks whose only commodity is money. An increasing number of them are forming clubs of one description or another which afford members no-fee checking accounts, discounted loan rates, discounts on safety deposit boxes, free traveler's checks and money orders, free notary service, new automobile discounts, pharmacy discounts, and discounted travel services.

Many banks which do not have a club offer some of these benefits to seniors. If you're not receiving these from your bank, ask what they have available. If you're not satisfied with the reply, shop around and compare.

BUSES

Greyhound Lines allows a 10% discount to seniors Monday through Thursday, and 5% Friday through Sunday. These discounts apply anywhere in the US that Greyhound operates. Gray Line Tours (an association of local independent tour operators) has a 15% discount policy in some areas for members of AARP. Check with Gray Line in the city you plan to visit to see whether it applies there.

Many local and regional bus lines have special fares for senior citizens (some are even free!). As with anything else, always ask about special prices. Most of them won't volunteer the information.

ENTERTAINMENT

Movie theater chains such as Edwards, Mann and United Artists, as well as many independent theaters, give seniors a substantial discount on tickets. There may be restrictions on performance times in some cases, so check with the movie houses in your community regarding ticket prices and conditions.

Some legitimate theaters and music centers have seniors programs, although at these you may have to wait in line until a few minutes before starting time because the number of reduced price tickets available will often depend on the number of unsold general tickets. Here again, check in advance.

HOTELS AND MOTELS

Unless you can get a better deal under one of the 50% off programs discussed in Chapter 11, you should take advantage of discounts offered by one of the many hotels, motels and resorts with special seniors programs. The amount of discount varies from one company to another, and sometimes depends on the season and whether it is a weekday or weekend. In some cases, you must be a member of one the seniors organizations to qualify for discounted rates. Request full details before making a reservation.

Following is a representative list of hostelries (which we do not represent to be complete) having some type of special rate structure for senior citizens. The list of hotels and motels which have seniors plans is constantly changing, so if the place you would like to stay is not shown here, check with them by telephone. Most of them an 800 number listed in the yellow pages.

Best Western, Compri Hotels, Clarion Hotels and Resorts, Comfort Inns, Days Inn, Doubletree Hotels, Drury Inns, Econo Lodges, Economy Inns of America, Econo-Travel Motor Hotels, Embassy Suites Hotels, Hampton Inns, Hilton Hotels, Holiday Inns, Howard Johnson, Hyatt Hotels, Imperial 400 Inns, Inn Suites, Knights Inn/Arborgate, La Quinta Motor Inns, LK Motels, Mariott, Master Hosts Inns, Mendel's, Omni Hotels, Quality Inns, Raddison Hotels, Ramada Inns, Red Carpet Inns, Red Lion Inns, Red Roof Inns, Relax Inns, Rodeway Inns, Sandman Hotels and Inns, Sheraton Hotels, Scottish Inns, Shoney's Inns, Sonesta International Hotels, Stouffer Hotels, Thunderbird Motor Hotels, Travelodge/Viscount, Treadway Inns, Vagabond Inns, Westin Hotels and Resorts, Westmark Hotels.

ANOTHER SOURCE

You can obtain a copy of The Mature Traveler's *1991 Survey of Lodging Deals* by writing to The Mature Traveler, P. O. Box 50820, Reno, NV 89513. The cost for this directory is $4.00. It lists the major chains which offer senior discounts, and gives the toll-free 800 telephone number for each.

NATIONAL OUTDOOR ATTRACTIONS

Residents of the United States who are 62 or older qualify for a "Golden Age Passport." This is a free lifetime pass to all national parks, wildlife refuges, recreation areas, monuments and other historic sites. These passports may be obtained at any National Park or National Wildlife Refuge. In addition to free admission to these attractions, passport holders also receive a 50% discount on such things as parking, boating, and tours.

For information on the hundreds of Government-owned attractions which may be visited on your Golden Age Passport, write to the following:

National Park Service, U. S. Department of the Interior, 18th & C Streets NW, Washington, DC 20240.

National Wildlife Refuges, c/o U. S. Fish and Wildlife Service, Department of the Interior, Washington, DC 20240.

U. S. Department of Agriculture Forest Service, P. O. Box 96090, Washington, DC 20090.

State Parks and Recreation Areas: To obtain information on special deals for seniors at the many state parks and recreation facilities, write to the Tourist Office at the state capitol of the state you plan to visit. You can get the address by calling the reference desk of your local public library.

RAILWAY FARES

Amtrak grants a 25% discount to passengers 65 or older except during certain periods around major holidays. Be prepared to prove your age. At times Amtrak may have special fares which are lower than the set senior fares, so it pays to check before purchasing your ticket.

For foreign rail travel, the following countries have some form of special rail ticket pricing for senior passengers: **Austria, Belgium, Canada, Denmark, Finland, France, Germany, Great Britain, Greece, Ireland, Italy, Luxembourg, the Netherlands, Norway, Portugal, Spain,**

Sweden, and Switzerland. Ages to qualify, prices, terms and conditions vary from country to country. Check with your travel agent or the US tourist office of the particular country or countries in which you will be traveling for full details.

Caution: If you plan to travel in more than one European country, you may be better off with a Eurailpass which is good for unlimited rail travel in several countries throughout Europe (Great Britain not included). There is no discount for seniors, but even so prices may be lower than buying senior passes for individual countries. Eurailpass prices depend on the period of travel time covered. Check with **Eurailpass,** P. O. Box 10383, Stamford, CT 06904-2383 or your travel agent for complete information.

RESTAURANTS AND CAFETERIAS

Many of the better known restaurant and fast-food chains allow a 10% discount to seniors, as do regional cafeteria chains and even some independent eateries. Most of these don't require that you be a member of any organization, and most don't ask for proof of age—unless you appear to be cheating. If you don't know whether a particular cafe or cafeteria has a senior discount, ask, otherwise you may never know.

SHOPPING

For special deals at the big retailers, Sears and Montgomery Ward, see the paragraphs on Seniors Organizations which follow. These two are probably the largest retailers which allow discounts to the 50 and over crowd, but they are not the only ones. As with anything else, get in the habit of asking "do you have a senior citizen's discount?" when shopping for everything.

SENIOR CITIZENS ORGANIZATIONS

There are a number of organizations which have been formed in the U. S. to promote the interests of senior citizens. Some of them are basically advocacy groups which concentrate on political causes and similar matters. Others also do this, but in addition have made arrangements for special prices on a variety of goods and services for their members. The range of services varies from one organization to another, so it is a good idea to obtain full information from each of them and compare benefits and costs before deciding which one (or more) to join.

When obtaining offers from companies affiliated with a seniors group, always compare prices and discounts from other sources. Just because a company has a tie-in with a seniors organization, or advertises in its publications, is no guarantee that it has the best deal around.

American Association of Retired Persons (AARP): Open to anyone who has arrived at his or her 50th birthday. Members receive subscriptions to *Modern Maturity* magazine and the *AARP News Bulletin*; lodging, car rental and sightseeing discounts; free booklets on retirement subjects; a nonprofit pharmacy service; a group travel program; an investment program; and possible savings in health, life and auto insurance.

Membership fees in AARP are $5 for one year or $12.50 for three years. A ten-year membership is available for $35, or a lifetime membership for $75. All prices include husband and wife. To join or to request further information, contact American Association of Retired Persons, 3200 Carson Street, Lakewood, CA 90712, telephone (213) 496-2277. Collect calls are accepted.

Mature Outlook: The qualification age for this Sear's owned operation is also 50 and up (your spouse can be any age). The membership fee is $9.95 for husband and wife, which includes subscriptions to *Mature Outlook Magazine* and *Mature Outlook Newsletter*.

Members receive discount coupons good at Sears stores and automotive centers, 10% off the membership fee in Sears' Allstate Motor Club, discounts on mail-order pharmacy items, and reduced prices on eyeglasses. A travel service and free traveler's checks are available. Also included are rental car discounts, and 20% off on Holiday Inn Rooms and 10% off on Holiday Inn meals. For information, contact Mature Outlook, P. O. Box 1208, Glenview, IL 60025-9935, or call (800) 366-6330.

Montgomery Ward Y.E.S. Discount Club: Open to persons of 50 and up, members of the Y.E.S. club receive a 10% discount off all Montgomery Ward merchandise on Tuesday of each week (even from sale prices), and the same discount for certain auto services on Tuesdays, Wednesdays, and Thursdays. Special deals are also available on hotels and motels, cars and rentals, airline fares, pharmacy items, traveler's checks (no fee), and cruises and tours.

The membership fee of $34.80 per year per couple may be paid monthly, if desired. It includes a subscription to the quarterly magazine *Vantage*. Contact the Montgomery Ward Y.E.S. Discount Club, 200 N. Martingale Road, Schaumburg, IL 60194. Toll-free telephone numbers are (800) 621-4797 for Illinois callers, or (800) 421-5396 from other areas.

National Council of Senior Citizens: This is primarily an advocacy group with its major emphasis being on political and policy matters which affect senior citizens. However, it does have arrangements for discounts on pharmacy items, travel, and some insurance. Dues are $8.00 per year. Contact NCSC at 925 15th Street NW, Washington, DC 20005, telephone (202) 347-8800.

National Alliance of Senior Citizens, Inc.: Along the same lines as the NCSC described above, this is basically a politically oriented lobbying group. Special prices for seniors are provided on new cars, car rentals, hotels and motels, prescription drugs, and vitamins & minerals. Travel services are offered. Dues are $10.00 per year for an individual, or $15.00 for husband and wife. For more information, write to the National Alliance of Senior Citizens, 2525 Wilson Boulevard, Arlington, VA 22202, or call them at (703) 528-4380.

The Retired Officers Association: As the name would indicate, this organization is open only to people who have been an officer in one of the U. S. military services. No age limit is specified, as long as you meet the "retired officer" description. Like the other organizations listed above, the ROA is involved in political lobbying, but it has discount arrangements for car rentals, hotels and motels, medical prescriptions, group health and life insurance, and special deals on foreign travel. Dues are $16.00 per year. Contact this organization at 201 N. Washington Street, Alexandria, VA 22314, telephone (703) 549-2311.

ADDITIONAL INFORMATION

For details on other goodies available to folks who have hit the half-century mark, including educational opportunities, sporting events, national and state parks, and miscellaneous activities, check out the following books at your local library or order them from the publisher or through your bookstore:

Golden Opportunities - Deals & Discounts for Senior Citizens, (price $9.95) published by Thomasson-Grant, One Morton Drive, Suite 500, Charlottesville, VA 22901.

Unbelievably Good Deals & Great Adventures That You Absolutely Can't Get Unless You're Over 50, by Joan Rattner Heilman, published by Contemporary Books, Inc., 180 N, Michigan Avenue, Chicago, IL 60601. (Price $7.95 plus 3.95 s&h).

Chapter 26

LIBRARIES - NEGLECTED TREASURE TROVES

One of the greatest bargains available to consumers—and one of our most under-used resources—is the nation's library systems. According to the *American Library Directory*, published by R. R. Bowker Company, there are approximately 30,000 libraries in the United States. This number includes 15,000 public libraries and branches, almost 5000 university and college libraries, and about 10,000 special libraries including those operated by Government and the armed forces.

The *Directory of Special Libraries and Information Centers*, published by Gale Research, Inc., lists more than 19,800 Special Libraries, Research Libraries, Information Centers, Archives, and Data Centers. This number takes into account university and college libraries counted separately by Bowker, plus a number of centers not usually considered to be libraries by the average layman.

Services provided by libraries are greater and more varied than most people realize, and for the most part they are free. That is, they are free to the extent that they have been prepaid by the public in the form of taxes, or by some sponsoring organization, and are there waiting to be used. Failure to take full advantage of these facilities is not only a waste of resources, it represents missed opportunities for considerable money savings by individuals.

According to an article in the December 17, 1990 issue of *The Christian Science Monitor*, libraries across the country have been staggering—and even collapsing—for lack of local support. This situation is no doubt due in large part to lack of knowledge by the public of the services and benefits offered by libraries, and of how easy it is to take advantage of these features. This is in spite of the fact that many libraries go to great length to promote public awareness of their existence and resources.

A book on how to save money on just about everything would not be complete if it didn't bring attention to the savings available to everyone through our library systems. This is true not only for people who like to read a lot, but also for business people who need to do research, for individual investors who would like to have access to well-known information and advisory services without paying expensive subscription fees, for students doing school research, for young children with an insatiable appetite for story books, and for anyone else interested in an inexpensive source of enlightenment and entertainment.

PUBLIC LIBRARIES

You will notice throughout this book that when we recommend a source of information on a particular subject, we often say "check with your local public library." Almost everyone is familiar to some extent with public libraries. This is the place the average person usually thinks of when the word "library" is mentioned.

As noted, there are about 15,000 public libraries in the U.S., including branches. Public libraries are those established and supported by some unit of government: state, city, town, county, etc. They are the libraries most accessible to the average citizen because branches are spread throughout the local area. They are also normally the libraries of greatest interest to the him because they cater to his needs and wants rather than to specialized audiences.

The range of materials and services available varies from one library system to another, and from one branch to another. However, the basic offerings will be quite similar. Many systems are set up so that inter-branch transfers of assets are possible upon request. Where such transfers are not possible, your local branch should be able to tell you which branch is likely to have the book, directory, periodical, newspaper, tape, video, or other item you require.

If you are not a regular library patron, it would be well worth your while to go to your local public library and spend one or two hours just poking around to see what is there. Explore the bookshelves, check out the magazine and newspaper racks, look over the reference books, directories, videos and audio tapes. Ask the librarian to explain the computer, microfiche, copying and other equipment on hand.

Some libraries hold sessions in which they teach patrons how to use the library and its facilities. Ask about this. These informal sessions are free of charge and extremely helpful.

General Readers: How much money can you save using libraries? Answer: Lots. For example, the average price for hard-back books today is about $27.00. Lets say you would like to read at least one book a month from a best-seller list. By borrowing these books from your library instead of buying them, your annual savings on this alone would amount to over $300!

Of course, once you start using the library on a regular basis you probably won't stop at one book a month, but may start reading two or three, or using the library's magazine list, or audio and video inventory, or other services and facilities.

Most libraries carry the latest hard-cover best-sellers, whether fiction or non fiction, plus thousands of older volumes including a large selection of children's books. There are very few subjects on which you would not be able to find a book or periodical at your local public library or somewhere in the library system of your city or county.

For the Gourmet: Are you a nut about cook books, but can't afford to buy as many as you would like? Browse through the cook book section of the closest library. You will find dozens, if not hundreds, of recipe books of every description including ethnic, diet, regional, foreign, food type, dietary preference, cooking style, and so on. You could have a constantly revolving cook book library on your kitchen shelf by checking out different books each month.

Young Readers: Do you have young children whom you would like to get interested in reading, or whose voracious reading appetites already are breaking your budget? The children's bookshelves at your local library may be your answer in either case.

For the Traveler: Planning a vacation? You will find several good travel books by recognized travel writers at your local library. Many libraries also have video travel cassettes of various countries, regions and cities around the world.

Information Please: Need a piece of information fast and don't know where to turn? Call the reference section of your library. If the answer can be found in their vast storehouse of reference works, they will cheerfully get it for you. They are used to all kinds of queries. Some libraries have networks which they can use to get information from distant sources if they can't provide it locally.

Investors: For the investor, many public libraries provide a wide range of financial and advisory publications, most of which are quite expensive if ordered on an individual basis.

As an example, the public library system in the county in which the author presently resides provides the following resources under the heading **Investment Advisory Tools**: *Daily Graphs Stock Options Guide, Moody's Bond Survey, Rate%Gram, Standard & Poor's Credit Week, Standard & Poor's Outlook, Standard & Poor's Trendline Stock Chart Services, The Bank Quarterly Ratings & Analysis, The S&L Quarterly Ratings & Analysis, Value Line Investment Survey*, and the *Wall Street Transcript*.

In addition, the following financial data publications are carried under the heading **Investment Information Sources**: *Daily Stock Price Record, Directory of Obsolete Securities, Donoghue's Mutual Fund Almanac, Dow Jones No-Load Mutual Fund Profiles, Lotus One Source, Moody's Dividend Record, Moody's Handbook of Common Stocks, Moody's*

Manuals, Moody's Handbook of OTC Stocks, Moody's Manuals on Microfiche, Moody's Market Comment, Mutual Fund Sourcebook, Nelson's Directory of Investment Managers, Nelson's Guide to Neglected Stocks, New York Stock Exchange Guide, Q-File, Standard & Poor's Bond Guide, Standard & Poor's Corporation Records, Standard & Poor's Dividend Records, Standard & Poor's/Lipper Mutual Fund Profiles, Standard & Poor's Security Dealers of North America, Standard & Poor's Stock Guide, Standard & Poor's Stock Market Encyclopedia, Standard & Poor's Stock Reports, Weisenberger Investment Companies Services.

Your library may not have all the publications listed above—they are usually spread throughout the system—but will probably have the more popular ones. Using just two or three of these guides at your library, rather than subscribing to them, could save you hundreds of dollars in annual subscription prices.

Researchers: Whether you are a student, business person, or just an average reader with an interest in a particular field, the research tools available at libraries—public and special—are impressive, indeed. These tools include not only the data bases available in the form of books, directories, magazines, newspapers, and other periodicals, but sophisticated computer and other equipment which enable users to quickly and easily identify and locate the information needed.

There are a number of ways to go about researching a given subject, but the best way is to start at the source—that is, determine just where you should start looking. Almost all libraries have reference books to use as a starting point. Many of them even have reference books on reference books.

Tell your librarian the subject in which your are interested and ask her to provide you with a list of reference books or directories on the subject. Most of these will be for use only in the library—you will not be able to check them out. But, then, you don't need to. All you are looking for at this point is information to set you on the right path.

If you want to see whether the subject you are researching has been covered by an article in one or more periodicals, you should start by looking in the *Reader's Guide to Periodical Literature* which practically every library will have.

For newspaper articles, whether recent or going back many years, most libraries have a complete file on microfiche tape of one or more major local newspapers plus a selection of well-known national or international papers such as the *Christian Science Monitor*, the *Los Angeles Times*, the *New York Times*, the *Times* (of London), and *The Wall Street Journal*.

If you are interested in learning more about using libraries for research, attend one of the short training sessions mentioned earlier which are open to the public. Ask for information on these at your library.

A good book on the subject is *Finding Facts Fast* (sub-title: *How to Find Out What You want and Need to Know)*, by Alden Todd published by Ten Speed Press. Check your local library, or order from the publisher at P. O. Box 7123, Berkeley, CA 94707 (paperback $3.95 plus .75 p&h, or clothbound $7.95 plus 1.00 p&h).

SPECIAL LIBRARIES

As mentioned at the beginning of this chapter, the *Directory of Special Libraries and Information Centers*, published by Gale Research Inc., lists almost 20,000 special libraries, research libraries, information centers, archives, and data centers maintained by government agencies, business, industry, newspapers, educational institutions, nonprofit organizations, and societies in the fields of science & engineering, medicine, law, art, religion, the social sciences, and humanities. There are even libraries for the blind and physically handicapped.

If you cannot find all the information you need on a given subject at your local library, ask the reference desk person if she can recommend another library source nearby. If not, consult the Gale directory (above) or the *American Library Directory,*

published by R. R. Bowker.   Local university or college
libraries, in particular, offer excellent research facilities.

U. S. GOVERNMENT DEPOSITORY LIBRARIES

These are libraries within the Special Library listing devoted
to U. S. Government documents.   They are covered in detail in
Chapter 27 *U. S. Government Publications.*

Chapter 27

U. S. GOVERNMENT PUBLICATIONS

You may be under the impression that Uncle Sam's printing presses stay busy 24 hours a day doing nothing but churning out currency to replace worn-out dollar bills, and printing larger bills to pay interest on the national debt. This is not quite true.

The Federal Government, through the U. S. Government Printing Office (GPO) and its primary distributor, the Superintendent of Documents, is the nation's largest provider of information publications. It employs more than 5000 people, has about 20,000 titles in its inventory, operates 24 bookstores, runs a giant mail-order business, and brings in approximately one *billion* dollars in sales revenue each year.

The three branches of government—executive, legislative, and judicial—are constantly generating documents which must be printed and made available to the public. Under federal law, the GPO is responsible for printing and distributing these documents.

In addition, various agencies of the government publish and distribute documents which are not made available through the Superintendent of Documents. These are generally (but not always) publications relating to technical or highly specialized fields not of interest to the average consumer.

If you are interested in information on a subject not listed in one of the GPO catalogs mentioned below, ask a librarian at the closest U. S. Government Depository Library (see information later in this chapter) for help in tracking it down. Chances are it can be located somewhere. There is hardly a subject that some government agency hasn't covered in a publication.

CATALOGS

Government publications are listed in a variety of catalogs which may be found at U. S. Government Bookstores, Federal

Depository Libraries, or (in some cases), local libraries. Catalogs may also be requested from the Superintendent of Documents, U. S. Government Printing Office, Washington, DC 20402, or as noted below. The more popular catalogs are:

Census Catalog and Guide (item #138) (annually), published by the U. S. Department of Commerce, Bureau of the Census, but available from the Superintendent of Documents.

Consumer Information Catalog (quarterly), available free of charge from the Consumer Information Center, P. O. Box 100, Pueblo, CO 81002.

Monthly Catalog of U. S. Government Publications (item #557-A)

New Books catalog (item #556-B) (bimonthly)

Publications Available from GPO (item #968-H-15)

U. S. Government Books (item #556-A) (quarterly)

To give you an idea of the scope of publications offered by the GPO, a recent *Consumer Information Catalog* listed brochures on the following topics: careers, cars, children, education, federal programs, food, health, housing, money management, small business, travel & hobbies, and miscellaneous sources of assistance. Many of these are free, others are priced from fifty cents to $5.00.

BOOKS

A *New Books* catalog for the same period listed titles in the fields of agriculture, business & labor, the census, federal regulations, computers & computer science, consumer topics, education, energy & the environment, health, international topics, law & law enforcement, military, national topics, public administration, public laws, science, transportation, and miscellaneous. Prices ranged from a low of $1.00 to a high of $42.00, with most items being under $5.00.

Titles listed in the current catalog of *U. S. Government Books*, which carries those published prior to the ones listed in the *New Books* catalog, covered many of the same subjects mentioned in the above paragraph plus several others. The price range was similar.

ORDERING INFORMATION

Whether ordering from the Superintendent of Documents in Washington, the Consumer Information Center in Pueblo, or any U. S. Government Bookstore, payment may be by personal check, VISA, MasterCard, or deposit account. A deposit account is a prepaid account established by regular buyers by depositing a minimum of $50.00 with the GPO. Write to Superintendent of Documents, Deposit Accounts Section, Stop: SSOR, U. S. Government Printing Office, Washington, DC, (or call 202-783-3238) for information.

A directory of U. S. Government Bookstores is printed at the end of this chapter.

U. S. GOVERNMENT DEPOSITORY LIBRARIES

The purpose of the depository library program is to make available to the public all Government publications except those determined to be for official use only, those classified for reasons of national security, and others which are determined to have no public interest or educational value.

There are approximately 1400 depository libraries in the United States. They are located in every state in the union, and in every Congressional District in each state. Considering that the depository library system was established by an act of Congress, this is not too surprising. Depository libraries may be attached to public libraries, college or university libraries, military or other government libraries, law libraries, or other special libraries.

There is not space in this book to list the 1400 libraries making up this system. You can get the addresses of those nearest you by contacting your local public library, or by requesting *A Directory of U. S. Government Depository Libraries* from the Superintendent of Documents, U. S. Government Printing Office, Washington, DC 20402.

U. S. GOVERNMENT BOOK STORES

See the pages which follow for a complete list of U. S. Government Book Stores.

DIRECTORY OF U. S. GOVERNMENT BOOKSTORES

ALABAMA
O'Neill Building
2021 Third Avenue, North
Birmingham, AL 35203
(205-731-1056)

CALIFORNIA
ARCO Plaza, C-Level
505 South Flower Street
Los Angeles, CA 90071
(213-239-9844)

Room 1023, Federal Building
450 Golden Gate Avenue
San Francisco, CA 94102
(415-252-5334)

COLORADO
Room 117 Federal Building
1961 Stout Street
Denver, CO 80294
(303-844-3964)

World Savings Building
720 North Main Street
Pueblo, CO 81003
(719-544-3142)

DISTRICT OF COLUMBIA
U. S. Gov't Printing Office
710 North Capitol Street, NW
Washington, DC 20401
(202-275-2091)

1510 H Street, NW
Washington, DC 20005
(202-653-5075)

FLORIDA
Room 158 Federal Building
400 W. Bay Street
Jacksonville, FL 32202
(904-353-0569)

GEORGIA
Room 100 Federal Building
275 Peachtree Street, NE
P. O. Box 56445
Atlanta, GA 30343
(404-331-6947)

ILLINOIS
Room 1365 Federal Building
219 S. Dearborn Street
Chicago, IL 60604
(312-353-5133)

MARYLAND
Warehouse Sales Outlet
8660 Cherry Lane
Laurel, MD 20707
(301-953-7974)
(301-792-0262)

MASSACHUSETTS
Thomas P. O'Neill Building
10 Causeway Street
Room 179
Boston, MA 02222
(617-720-4180)

MICHIGAN
Suite 160 Federal Building
477 Michigan Avenue
Detroit, MI 48226
(313-226-7816)

MISSOURI
120 Bannister Mall
5600 E. Bannister Road
Kansas City, MO 64137
(816-765-2256)

NEW YORK
Room 110
26 Federal Plaza
New York, NY 10278
(212-264-3825)

OHIO
Room 1653 Federal Building
1240 E. 9th Street
Cleveland, OH 44199
(216-522-4922)

Room 207 Federal Building
200 N. High Street
Columbus, OH 43215
(614-469-6956)

OREGON
1305 S. W. First Avenue
Portland, OR 97201-5801
(503-221-6217)

PENNSYLVANIA
Robert Morris Building
100 North 17th Street
Philadelphia, PA 19103
(215-597-0677)

PENNSYLVANIA (Cont'd)
Room 118 Federal Building
1000 Liberty Avenue
Pittsburgh, PA 15222
(412-644-2721)

TEXAS
Room 1C46 Federal Building
1100 Commerce Street
Dallas, TX 75242
(214-767-0076)

Texas Crude Building
801 Travis Street
Suite 120
Houston, TX 77002
(713-228-1187)

WASHINGTON
Room 194 Federal Building
915 Second Avenue
Seattle, WA 98174
(206-442-4270)

WISCONSIN
Room 190 Federal Building
517 E. Wisconsin Avenue
Milwaukee, WI 53202
(414-297-1304)

Chapter 28

CONSUMER PROTECTION AGENCIES

Consumers have the right to expect quality products and services at fair prices. They also have the right to receive what they pay for, and to expect sellers to stand behind their products if a problem develops. However, every transaction doesn't turn out as expected by the buyer. This is not surprising, considering the millions of transactions that occur in the market place each day.

WHEN THINGS GO WRONG

Most sellers make an effort to settle customer complaints in a satisfactory manner—not just because it's the right thing to do, but also because it's good business.

Sometimes, however, complaints don't get handled to the satisfaction of the customer. The reason may be because of an honest difference of opinion between buyer and seller over terms of the sale, or because of dishonesty, irresponsibility, red tape or just plain stubbornness on the part of the merchant.

Federal and state governments have many laws on the books for the protection of consumers. These governments—along with county and city governments in some cases—have established offices to assist consumers with problems which they have not been able to resolve themselves.

Where To Turn: Following in this section are two lists. The first list covers Federal Information Centers. These are offices which help consumers find information about federal services, programs and regulations. They can also direct consumers to the proper federal agency for help with problems which might be covered by federal law.

The second list covers State Consumer Protection Offices. The consumer would normally turn to the state offices first, especially if the dispute or problem involved an in-state vendor.

In some states, counties and cities have similar offices of their own for dealing with strictly local problems. Due to space limitations, we are unable to include those in this book. You can obtain information on these from your state agency, or from the publication mentioned below.

The lists which follow were taken from the *Consumer's Resource Handbook*, published by the United States Office of Consumer Affairs, available from the Consumer Information Center, Pueblo, CO 81009. Single copies are free of charge. This booklet has much useful information in addition to the lists contained herein, including listings of corporate consumer contacts, auto manufacturers, Better Business Bureaus, trade associations, and various federal and state agencies.

We have included this section in *How to Save Money on Just About Everything* because resolving a problem on something you have purchased, rather than having to replace it or have it repaired at your own expense, will certainly save money.

FEDERAL INFORMATION CENTERS

ALABAMA
Birmingham
(205) 322-8591
Mobile
(205) 438-1421

ALASKA
Anchorage
(907) 271-3650

ARIZONA
Phoenix
(602) 261-3313

ARIZONA
Little Rock
(501) 378-6177

CALIFORNIA
Los Angeles
(213) 894-3800
Sacramento
(916) 551-2380
San Diego
(619) 557-6030
San Francisco
(415) 556-6600
Santa Ana
(714) 836-2386

COLORADO
Colorado Springs
(303) 471-9491
Denver
(303) 844-6575
Pueblo
(303) 544-9523

CONNECTICUT
Hartford
(203) 527-2617
New Haven
(203) 624-4720

FLORIDA
Ft. Lauderdale
(305) 522-8531
Jacksonville
(904) 354-4756
Miami
(305) 536-4155
Orlando
(305) 422-1800
St. Petersburg
(813) 893-3495
Tampa
(813) 229-7911
West Palm Beach
(305) 833-7566

GEORGIA
Atlanta
(404) 331-6891

HAWAII
Honolulu
(808) 551-1365

ILLINOIS
Chicago
(312) 353-4242

INDIANA
Gary
(219) 883-4110
Indianapolis
(317) 269-7373

FEDERAL INFORMATION CENTERS

IOWA
All Points
(800) 532-1556

KANSAS
All Points
(800) 432-2934

KENTUCKY
Louisville
(502) 582-6261

LOUISIANA
New Orleans
(504) 589-6696

MARYLAND
Baltimore
(301) 962-4980

MASSACHUSETTS
Boston
(617) 565-8121

MICHIGAN
Detroit
(313) 226-7016
Grand Rapids
(616) 451-2628

MINNESOTA
Minneapolis
(612) 370-3333

MISSOURI
St. Louis
(314) 425-4106
Other Missouri
(800) 392-7711

NEBRASKA
Omaha
(402) 221-3353
Other Nebraska
(800) 642-8383

NEW JERSEY
Newark
(201) 645-3600
Trenton
(609) 396-4400

NEW MEXICO
Albuquerque
(505) 766-3091

NEW YORK
Albany
(518) 463-4421
Buffalo
(716) 846-4010
New York
(212) 264-4464
Rochester
(716) 546-5075
Syracuse
(315) 476-8545

**NORTH
CAROLINA**
Charlotte
(704) 376-3600

OHIO
Akron
(216) 375-5638
Cincinnati
(513) 684-2801
Cleveland
(216) 522-4040

FEDERAL INFORMATION CENTERS

OHIO (Cont'd)
Columbus
  (614) 221-1014
Dayton
  (513) 223-7377
Toledo
  (419) 241-3223

OKLAHOMA
Oklahoma City
  (405) 231-4868
Tulsa
  (918) 584-4193

OREGON
Portland
  (503) 221-2222

PENNSYLVANIA
Philadelphia
  (215) 597-7042
Pittsburgh
  (412) 644-3456

RHODE ISLAND
Providence
  (401) 331-5565

TENNESSEE
Chattanooga
  (615) 265-8231
Memphis
  (901) 521-3285
Nashville
  (615) 242-5056

TEXAS
Austin
  (512) 472-5494

TEXAS (Cont'd)
Dallas
  (214) 767-8585
Fort Worth
  (817) 334-3624
Houston
  (713) 229-2552
San Antonio
  (512) 224-4471

UTAH
Salt Lake City
  (801) 524-5353

VIRGINIA
Norfolk
  (804) 441-3101
Richmond
  (804) 643-4928
Roanoke
  (703) 982-8591

WASHINGTON
Seattle
  (206) 442-0570
Tacoma
  (206) 383-5230

WISCONSIN
Milwaukee
  (414) 271-2273

STATE CONSUMER PROTECTION OFFICES

ALABAMA
Consumer Protection Division
Office of Attorney General
11 South Union Street
Montgomery, AL 36130
(205) 261-7334
(800) 392-5658

ALASKA
Consumer Protection Section
Office of Attorney General
1031 West Fourth Ave, Ste 110
Anchorage, AK 99501
(907) 279-0428

Investigator
Office of Attorney General
100 Cushman St, Ste 400
Fairbanks, AK 99701
(907) 456-8588

AMERICAN SAMOA
Consumer Protection Bureau
P. O. Box 7
Pago Pago, AQ 96799
(684) 633-1786 (on island)
(684) 663-4163

ARIZONA
Financial Fraud Division
Office of Attorney General
1275 West Washington St
Phoenix, AZ 85007
(602) 255-3702 (fraud only)
(800) 352-8431

Financial Fraud Division
Office of Attorney General
402 West Congress St, Ste 315
Tucson, AZ 85701
(602) 628-5501

ARKANSAS
Consumer Protection Division
Office of Attorney General
201 East Markham Street
Little Rock, AR 72201
(501) 371-2341 (voice/TDD)
(800) 482-8982 (voice/TDD)

CALIFORNIA
Dept. of Consumer Affairs
1020 N Street
Sacramento, CA 95814
(916) 445-0660 (complaints)
(916) 445-1254 (information)
(916) 322-1700 (TDD)

Dept. of Consumer Affairs
107 S. Broadway, Room 8020
Los Angeles, CA 90012
(213) 620-4360
(213) 620-2179 (TDD)

COLORADO
Consumer Protection Unit
Office of Attorney General
1525 Sherman St, 3rd Floor
Denver, CO 80203
(303) 866-5167

CONNECTICUT
Dept. of Consumer Protection
State Office Building
165 Capitol Avenue
Hartford, CT 06106
(203) 566-4999
(800) 842-2649

STATE CONSUMER PROTECTION OFFICES

DELAWARE
Division of Consumer Affairs
Dept. of Community Affairs
820 North French St, 4th Floor
Wilmington, DE 19801
(302) 571-3250

DISTRICT OF COLUMBIA
Department of Consumer and
Regulatory Affairs
614 H Street, N.W.
Washington, DC 20001
(202) 727-7000

FLORIDA
Department of Agriculture and
Consumer Services
Division of Consumer Services
508 Mayo Building
Tallahassee, FL 32399
(904) 488-2226
(800) 342-2176 (TDD)
(800) 327-3382

GEORGIA
Governor's Office of Consumer
Affairs
2 Martin Luther King Dr S.E.
Plaza Level - East Tower
Atlanta, GA 30334
(404) 656-7000
(800) 282-5808

HAWAII
Office of Consumer Protection
Department of Commerce and
  Consumer Affairs
250 S. King Street, Room 520
Honolulu, HI 96812
(808) 548-2540

HAWAII (Cont'd)
75 Aupuni Street
Hilo, HI 96720
(808) 961-7433

3060 Eiwa Street
Lihue, HI 96766
(808) 245-4365

54 High Street
Wailuku, HI 96793
(808) 244-4387

ILLINOIS
Governor's Office of Citizens
Assistance
201 West Monroe Street
Springfield, IL 62706
(217) 782-0244
(800) 642-3112

Consumer Protection Division
Office of Attorney General
100 West Randolph, 12th Floor
Chicago, IL 60601
(312) 917-3580
(312) 793-2852 (TDD)

Dept. of Citizens Rights
100 West Randolph, 12th Floor
Chicago, IL 60601
(312) 917-3289
(312) 793-2852 (TDD)

INDIANA
Consumer Protection Division
Office of Attorney General
219 State House
Indianapolis, IN 46204
(317) 232-6330
(800) 382-5516

STATE CONSUMER PROTECTION OFFICES

IOWA
Citizen's Aide/Ombudsman
515 East 12th Street
Des Moines, IA 50319
(515) 281-3592
(800) 358-5510

Consumer Protection Division
Office of Attorney General
1300 East Walnut St, 2nd Floor
Des Moines, IA 50319
(515) 281-5926

KANSAS
Consumer Protection Division
Office of Attorney General
Kansas Judicial Cntr, 2nd Flr
Topeka, KS 66612
(913) 296-3751
(800) 432-2310

KENTUCKY
Consumer Protection Division
Office of Attorney General
209 Saint Clair Street
Frankfort, KY 40601
(502) 564-2200
(800) 432-9257

514 W. Liberty St, Ste 139
Louisville, KY 40202
(502) 588-3262

LOUISIANA
Consumer Protection Section
Office of Attorney General
State Capitol Building
Baton Rouge, LA 70804
(504) 342-7013

LOUISIANA (Cont'd)
Agro-Consumer Services
Department of Agriculture
325 Loyola Ave, Room 317
New Orleans, LA 70012
(504) 568-5472

MAINE
Consumer and Antitrust Div.
Office of Attorney General
State House Station No. 6
Augusta, ME 04333
(207) 289-3716

Mediation Consumer Service
Office of Attorney General
991 Forest Avenue
Portland, ME 04104
(207) 797-8978

MARYLAND
Consumer Protection Division
Office of Attorney General
7 North Calvert Street
Baltimore, MD 21202
(301) 528-8662
(301) 576-6372 (TDD)
(301) 565-0451 (TDD)

State Office Complex
Route 50 and Cypress Street
Salisbury, MD 21801
(301) 543-6620

138 East Antietam St, Ste 210
Hagerstown, MD 21740
(301) 791-4780

STATE CONSUMER PROTECTION OFFICES

MASSACHUSETTS
Consumer Protection Division
Department of Attorney General
1 Ashburton Place, 19th Floor
Boston, MA 02108
(617) 727-8400

436 Dwight Street
Springfield, MA 01103
(413) 785-1951

MICHIGAN
Consumer Protection Division
Office of Attorney General
670 Law Building
Lansing, MI 48913
(517) 373-1140

Michigan Consumers Council
414 Hollister Building
106 West Allegan Street
Lansing, MI 48933
(517) 373-0947
(517) 737-0701 (TDD)

MINNESOTA
Office of Consumer Services
Office of Attorney General
117 University Avenue
St. Paul, MN 55155
(612) 296-2331

320 West Second Street
Duluth, MN 55802
(218) 723-4891

MISSISSIPPI
Consumer Protection Division
Office of Attorney General
P. O. Box 220
Jackson, MS 39205
(601) 354-6018
(601) 359-3680

MISSOURI
Trade Offense Division
Office of Attorney General
P. O. Box 899
Jefferson City, MO 65102
(314) 751-2616
(800) 393-8222

MONTANA
Consumers Affairs Unit
Department of Commerce
1424 Ninth Avenue
Helena, MT 59620
(406) 444-4312

NEBRASKA
Consumer Protection Division
Department of Justice
2115 State Capitol
Lincoln, NE 68509
(402) 471-2682

NEVADA
Commissioner of Consumer
Affairs
Department of Commerce
State Mail Room Complex
Las Vegas, NV 89158
(702) 486-4150

STATE CONSUMER PROTECTION OFFICES

NEVADA (Cont'd)
Consumer Affairs Division
201 Nye Bldg, Capitol Complex
Carson City, NV 86710
(702) 885-4340

NEW HAMPSHIRE
Antitrust Division
Office of Attorney General
State House Annex
Concord, NH 03301
(603) 271-3641

NEW JERSEY
Division of Consumer Affairs
1100 Raymond Blvd, Room 504
Newark, NJ 07102
(201) 648-4010

NEW MEXICO
Consumer and Economic Crime
   Division
Office of Attorney General
P. O. Box 1508
Santa Fe, NM
(505) 872-6910
(800) 432-2070

NEW YORK
New York State Consumer
   Protection Board
99 Washington Avenue
Albany, NY 12210
(518) 474-8583

250 Broadway, 17th Floor
New York, NY 10007
(212) 587-4482

NEW YORK (Cont'd)
Bureau of Consumer Frauds and
   Protection
Office of Attorney General
State Capitol
Albany, NY 12224
(518) 474-5481

120 Broadway
New York, NY 10271
(212) 341-2300

NORTH CAROLINA
Consumer Protection Section
Office of Attorney General
Dept. of Justice Building
Raleigh, NC 27602
(919) 733-7741

NORTH DAKOTA
Office of Attorney General
State Capitol Building
Bismarck, ND 58505
(701) 224-2210

OHIO
Consumer Frauds and Crimes
   Section
Office of Attorney General
30 East Broad Street
State Office Tower, 15th Flr
Columbus, OH 43266
(614) 466-8831
(800) 262-0515
(614) 466-1393 (TDD)

Consumers' Counsel
137 East State Street
Columbus, OH 43215
(614) 466-9605 (voice/TDD)
(800) 282-9448

STATE CONSUMER PROTECTION OFFICES

OKLAHOMA
Assistant Attorney General for
Consumer Affairs
Office of Attorney General
112 State Capitol Building
Oklahoma City, OK 73105
(405) 521-3921

Department of Consumer Credit
B82 Jim Thorpe Building
Oklahoma City, OK 73105
(405) 521-3653

OREGON
Financial Fraud Section
Department of Justice
Justice Building
Salem, OR 97310
(503) 378-4320

PENNSYLVANIA
Bureau of Consumer Protection
Office of Attorney General
Strawberry Square, 14th Floor
Harrisburg, PA 17120
(717) 787-9707
(717) 787-7109
(800) 441-2555

27 North Seventh Street
Allentown, PA 18101
(215) 821-6690
919 State Street, Room 203
Erie, PA 16501
(814) 4371

1009 State Office Building
1400 West Spring Garden Street
Philadelphia, PA 19130
(215) 560-2414

PENNSYLVANIA (Cont'd)
Manor Building, 4th Floor
564 Forbes Avenue
Pittsburgh, PA 15219
(412) 565-5135

State Office Bldg., Room 358
100 Lackawanna Avenue
Scranton, PA
(717) 963-4913

PUERTO RICO
Department Consumer Affairs
Minillas Station
P.O. Box 41059
Santurce, PR 00940
(809) 722-7555

RHODE ISLAND
Consumer Protection Division
Department of Attorney General
72 Pine Street
Providence, RI 02903
(401) 277-2104

Rhode Island Consumers'
Council
365 Broadway
Providence, RI 02909
(401) 277-2764

SOUTH CAROLINA
Consumer Fraud and Antitrust
Section
Office of Attorney General
P. O. Box 11549
Columbia, SC 29211
(803) 734-3970

STATE CONSUMER PROTECTION OFFICES

SOUTH CAROLINA (Cont'd)
Department of Consumer Affairs
P. O. Box 5757
Columbia, SC 29250
(803) 734-9452
(800) 922-1594

SOUTH DAKOTA
Division of Consumer Affairs
Office of Attorney General
Anderson Building
Pierre, SD 57501
(605) 773-4400

TENNESSEE
Antitrust and Consumer
  Protection Division
Office of Attorney General
450 James Robertson Parkway
Nashville, TN 37219
(615) 741-2672

Division of Consumer Affairs
Department of Commerce and
  Insurance
1808 West End Bldg, Ste 105
Nashville, TN 37219
(615) 741-4737
(800) 342-8385

TEXAS
Consumer Protection Division
Office of Attorney General
Capitol Sta., P.O. Box 12548
Austin, TX 78711
(512) 463-2070

Renaissance Place, 7th Floor
714 Jackson Street
Dallas, TX 75202
(214) 742-8944

TEXAS (Cont'd)
4824 Alberta Street, Ste 160
El Paso, TX 79905
(915) 533-3484

1001 Texas Avenue, Ste 700
Houston, TX 77002
(713) 223-5886

806 Broadway, Ste 312
Lubbock, TX 79401
(806) 747-5238

4309 North Tenth, Suite B
McAllen, TX 78501
(512) 682-4547

200 Main Plaza, Ste 400
San Antonio, TX 78205
(512) 225-4191

UTAH
Div. of Consumer Protection
Dept. of Business Regulation
160 East 300 South
Salt Lake City, UT 84145
(801) 530-6601

Assistant Attorney General for
  Consumer Affairs
130 State Capitol
Salt Lake City, UT 84114
(801) 533-5319

VERMONT
Public Protection Division
Office of Attorney General
109 State Street
Montpelier, VT 05602
(802) 828-3171

STATE CONSUMER PROTECTION OFFICES

VIRGIN ISLANDS
Consumer Services
  Administration
Golden Rock
Christiansted
St. Croix, VI 00820
(809) 774-3130

VIRGINIA
Division of Consumer Counsel
Office of Attorney General
Supreme Court Building
101 North Eighth Street
Richmond, VA 23219
(804) 786-2115

VIRGINIA (cont'd)
Office of Consumer Affairs
Room 101 Washington Bldg
1100 Bank Street
Richmond, VA 23219
(804) 786-2042
(800) 552-9963

100 N. Washington St, Ste 412
Falls Church, VA 22046
(703) 532-1613

WASHINGTON
Consumer and Business Fair
  Practices Division
Office of Attorney General
North 121 Capitol Way
Olympia, WA 98501
(206) 753-6210

1366 Dexter Horton Bldg
Seattle, WA 98104
(206) 464-7744
(800) 551-4636

WASHINGTON (Cont'd)
West 1116 Riverside Avenue
Spokane, WA 99201
(509) 456-3123

949 Market Street, Ste 380
Tacoma, WA 98402
(206) 593-2904

WEST VIRGINIA
Consumer Protection Division
Office of Attorney General
812 Quarrier St, 6th Floor
Charleston, WV 25301
(304) 348-8986
(800) 368-8808

WISCONSIN
Office of Consumer Protection
Department of Justice
P. O. Box 7856
Madison, WI 53707
(608) 266-1852
(800) 362-8189

Milwaukee State Office Bldg
819 N. 6th St, Room 520
Milwaukee, WI 53203
(414) 227-4948

Division of Trade and Consumer
  Protection
Department of Agriculture
801 West Badger Road
Madison, WI 53708
(608) 266-9836
(800) 362-3020

927 Loring Street
Altoona, WI 54720
(715) 839-3848

STATE CONSUMER PROTECTION OFFICES

WISCONSIN (Cont'd)
200 N. Jefferson St, Ste 146A
Green Bay, WI 54301
(414) 436-4087

10320 W. Silver Spring Drive
Milwaukee, WI 53225
(414) 438-4844

WYOMING
Office of Attorney General
123 State Capitol Building
Cheyenne, WY 82002
(307) 777-7841

ORDER FORM

To: Strebor Publications
P. O. Box 475
Laguna Beach, CA 92652

Please ship to me at the address below the following number of copies of *How To Save Money On Just About Everything.* Enclosed is my check or money order in the amount of $_____ which includes $2.00 (each) shipping and handling and 7.75% ($1.00 per book) California sales tax (tax applies to orders shipped to California only).

_____ copies @ $12.95 each $_____

Shipping & handling @ $2.00 each   _____

CA. sales tax @ $1.00 each   _____

TOTAL AMOUNT ENCLOSED   _____

Ship to:

Name_____

Address_____

City_____

State_____ Zip_____

ORDER FORM

To: Strebor Publications
P. O. Box 475
Laguna Beach, CA 92652

Please ship to me at the address below the following number of copies of *How To Save Money On Just About Everything.* Enclosed is my check or money order in the amount of $_____ which includes $2.00 (each) shipping and handling and 7.75% ($1.00 per book) California sales tax (tax applies to orders shipped to California only).

_____ copies @ $12.95 each $_____

Shipping & handling @ $2.00 each   _____

CA. sales tax @ $1.00 each   _____

TOTAL AMOUNT ENCLOSED   _____

Ship to:

Name_____

Address_____

City_____

State_____   Zip_____

ORDER FORM

To: Strebor Publications
P. O. Box 475
Laguna Beach, CA 92652

Please ship to me at the address below the following number of copies of *How To Save Money On Just About Everything.* Enclosed is my check or money order in the amount of $_____ which includes $2.00 (each) shipping and handling and 7.75% ($1.00 per book) California sales tax (tax applies to orders shipped to California only).

_____ copies @ $12.95 each	$_____
Shipping & handling @ $2.00 each	_____
CA. sales tax @ $1.00 each	_____
TOTAL AMOUNT ENCLOSED	_____

Ship to:

Name_____

Address_____

City_____

State_____ Zip_____